The Journey
from
Molestation and Promiscuity to a Triumphant Life in Christ
(Mr. A-Z and Finally, Me)

By Karen Wright

Published by
bpi
Blessed Pen Ink

©2018 by Karen Wright

All rights reserved. No portion of this book may be reproduced, stored in a retrieval system, or transmitted in any form or by any means-electronic, mechanical, photocopy, recording, scanning or other—except for brief quotations in critical reviews or articles, without the prior written permission of the publisher.

Published in Grand Rapids, Michigan, by Blessed Pen Ink, an imprint of Blessed Pen Ink Publishing.

Visit us at www.blessedpenink.com

Printed in the United States of America

Scripture taken from the HOLY BIBLE®, NEW INTERNATIONAL VERSION®. Copyright ©1973, 1978, 1984 by International Bible Society. Used by permission of Zondervan. All rights reserved.

Library of Congress Control Number:

ISBN-10   0-9740777-1-2
ISBN-13   978-0-9740777-1-0

Cover Graphic Design and Artwork by Blessed Pen Ink

This book is dedicated to my Lord and Savior, Jesus Christ, for making this project possible. Before salvation, I would always say, "If I write a book, it would be a number one seller!" As I grew in my Christian journey, the Holy Spirit began to impress upon my spirit to write. Soon, people in the body of Christ began to ask the question, "Are you writing a book?"

Well, needless to say, years later, I am being obedient to the assignment.

CONTENTS

FOREWORD ix

ACKNOWLEDGEMENTS xiii

INTRODUCTION xiv

Chapter One

In the Beginning... 1

    MR. A 5

    MR. B 7

    MR. C 10

    MR. D 23

    MR. E 29

    MR. F 29

    MR. G 33

Chapter Two

Moving On... 40

    MR. H 43

    MR. I 45

    MR. J 47

    MR. K 51

    MR. L 52

    MR. M 53

    MR. N 56

MR. O 62

Chapter Three

The Separation.. 66

    MR. P & MR. Q 67

    MR. R 69

    MR. S 69

    MR. T 70

    MR. U 71

Chapter Four

Captivity... 74

    MR. V 76

    MR. W 78

    MR. X 80

    MR. Y 83

Chapter Five

Freedom In the wrong way... 86

Chapter Six

The Shifting.. 94

    MR. Z 95

    MR. AB 97

    MR. AC 98

    MR. AD 100

Chapter Seven

Backslidden 102

    MR. AE 104

    MR. AF 108

Chapter Eight

The Shift 114

Chapter Nine

The Prodigal 118

    MR. AG 119

Chapter Ten

The End of a New Beginning 126

    JESUS' LOVE 127

    FINALLY, ME 130

    ABOUT THE AUTHOR 143

FOREWORD

I have had the honor and privilege of knowing Karen Wright for over a decade. When we met, I was a new babe in Christ. She had no idea about my past, just as I knew nothing of hers. Yet, she accepted me with open arms. I didn't know her but she had a familiar spirit. It was the spirit of God! I did not understand it at the time but speaking with her just felt like home. Our backgrounds were similar in some ways. I was molested, too and had my share of failed relationships because I was looking for love and trying to beat the "game of life". She was wise enough to give me a chance when others may have seen me as an outsider.

I would come to her when God would put something in my spirit or my dreams that I didn't totally understand and she would help me decipher His words and reasons. The bible says you can tell a true prophet when what they say comes to pass (Deuteronomy 18:20-22) and I can attest that Minister Wright truly is a Godsend. Everything she has shared with me has happened, even the marriage to my husband.

I was on my journey to discovering who and whose I was and she saw it all too clearly. In this book, she describes how God had a plan for her life and how He was molding her as a child for her purpose. It is so true! I can remember crying to her about some of my issues in marriage and her teaching me how to become a prayer warrior myself and how to bless my household and stand firm in the promises of God. The sharing of her testimony opened me to become stronger in Christ. Her story reveals so much of how she is able to maintain the strength she does when adversity approaches. Her power comes because of her experience and wisdom.

This book is so transparent and she is amongst my favorite authors in which I have been blessed to work with. Karen stayed the course, she listened, she learned and she made sacrifices for the love of her readers. I asked her to go into depth about very sensitive things in her life to place the reader in her feelings and she did it. I know it may have opened some old wombs but my prayer was that they were opened only to heal properly, not because of time but because they were properly cared for and cleaned.

When she first came to me about this book, she said God showed her my face in flames and she knew that He wanted her to seek my advice. She knew I was an author but had no idea that I started publishing, too. When I told her about my new company, you could hear her tears of joy through the phone. She was still following God, still letting Him direct her steps and still in Love with His goodness and grace. All I know is that her life is a prime example and shining light of grace extended. She is so brave and so forgiving. She still opens her heart, extends her love to her capturers, and holds no ill feelings. Her whole journey gives a fresh perspective of God's love and willingness to provide us with a clean slate no matter how dirty our lives have gotten.

I remember, Prophetess Wright speaking with a group of young women in a mentoring program. Her testimony had so many of them breaking chains of abuse and neglect. When you decide to walk in the way of God and stop shortcutting yourself out of life, you draw closer to a fantastic journey filled with love, life and the Light of Christ! You can hear the angels of God singing, "FREEDOM," from the heavens. This book, *Journey from Promiscuity and Molestation to a Triumphant Life in Christ: Mr. A-Z and Finally, Me,* is a map to true Love!

Forever in your debt,
Meochia Nochi Thompson

ACKNOWLEDGEMENTS

I want to Praise God for Meochia Nochi Thompson who is the Proprietor of Blessed Pen Ink that pushed and encouraged me to continue the God given assignment.

I also want to Praise God for my children, Shawntrice and Marques, who understand me and allow me to be me in the Body of Christ.

INTRODUCTION

The Journey through Molestation and Promiscuity to a Triumphant Life in Christ is a book of purpose to allow others who have gone through or are going through dark secrets in life a chance to heal. This book will help the reader open up and release inner hurt and pain in order to live the life God planned. A life with joy, peace and love and live in compassion and be a champion in spite of what life presented. It will also show how the chains of bondage were broken from man to man so that this young girl could come to know who she was in Christ who gave her life a new beginning.

This is a story about the struggles of a young girl who survived the hurt, rejection and pain from family secrets. However, in her life's journey, she begins to see how the struggles from her past made her victorious in Christ Jesus and was used an instrument towards her future. She also learned that the most important key to overcoming her life's obstacles was forgiveness of self and others.

I have loved you with an everlasting love. I have drawn you with an unfailing kindness. I will build you up again, and you, Virgin Israel, will be rebuilt (Jeremiah 31:3).

And when you stand praying, if you hold anything against anyone, forgive them, so that your Father in heaven may forgive you your sins (Mark 11:25).

Yes, Jesus proved His love to her in many capacities of her life, which made her whole and made her a "new creature in Christ".

The names of the men were changed to Mr. A through Mr. Z to symbolize the journey and because who they are is not as important as who I have become in Christ.

Chapter One

In the Beginning...

Childhood

I was living with my mom and both of my siblings on 67th and Parnell Avenue in Chicago, Illinois at the age of five. That building no longer exists. It was a basement apartment. I can remember the white pipes running in the ceiling. It was there, at Benjamin Banneker Public School, right down the street from our home, that I began my education. My mom worked nights to support us, so we stayed at home alone. "Latchkey kids" did not just start; it was something many single parents were doing long ago…lol.

Dad would come and pick us up for visitation on the weekends. I never like to bash men when families break up, especially when they are limited from seven days a week of seeing their children to two. All men do not fit the category of deadbeat dad but I do feel today's society allows men to think it is okay not to father their children when it doesn't hold them accountable.

You see, I am a product of a divorced home, which may not seem abnormal in today's society but you never realize the effect of it until you've been through the process. My mom and dad did a lot of arguing. I remember how I got excited when the weekends came because I loved my dad. Now, don't misunderstand me, I loved my mom, too but I saw her daily. Dad only came on the weekends and that is what made the difference. One time, a car hit me on a weekend visit! I was so excited to see my father that I just ran across the street to meet him without looking both ways. The car was speeding so fast down our block that it didn't have time to stop. When it hit me and I landed on its roof! Turned out, the driver was rushing their child to the hospital. Well, they ended up taking me, too.

My mom worked third shift at Spiegel's Catalog. She would instruct me not to open the door for anyone, every night. Well, disobedience costed me a journey that changed not only my life but my siblings, as well. (If there are any children reading this book, be obedient to your parents. You never know what it will cost you). My father came one night while my mom was at work, knocked on the door and I opened it. I really didn't know how bad my parent's relationship was. It was only later that I found out Dad was physically abusive towards my mom. She said he would beat her until she was black and blue. She not only wanted us to keep the doors shut from strangers, she was also closing out and protecting all of us from him. I didn't know. Well, that night, my dad took all three of us and that was the beginning of the journey of my life.

Elementary Years

That flight took us into a home on 62nd in Rhodes Avenue in Chicago, which we shared with my dad, his mom and my two uncles. Later in life, I found out that my youngest uncle was actually my cousin. This was an environment where children were not allowed in the building. We had to be extremely quiet and heaven forbid if my youngest sibling would cry. (That is what a baby does because that's their job, right?) Well, the adults didn't care that he cried because of his young age or because he missed his mother; when he cried, he would be scolded.

I recall not attending school because we traveled to my dad's home state of Virginia so much. I would consider this state our second home. It was a huge house with many rooms and there was a huge Oak tree in the backyard with a tire on it. That is where a lot of swinging went on...lol. It was where my father's Dad lived. He was a tall, dark skinned man. He was very handsome with a gentle heart but he was no joke. He was the disciplinarian of the family. Granddad didn't take no stuff. Grandmother lived in Chicago with her children because there was a separation between the two. It never dawned on me that they were not together or why. Being a kid, I guess I never thought to put the two together.

Soon, we moved to 57th in Aberdeen. My oldest uncle purchased the building. During this time, I was living with my oldest and youngest uncles, grandmother, dad and my two siblings on the second floor. There were seven people in one apartment. My uncle had the first bedroom; my grandma had the second bedroom. After that, the third bedroom belonged to Dad. I can't tell you where my youngest uncle and two brothers slept but I had a room with Grandmother.

MR. A

I feel like the enemy first came to destroy my life in this apartment! This is where the dark secret began. I was about seven or eight years old when the child molestation began. This was where Mr. A, my youngest uncle, began to lay me across the hassock (which we now call ottomans) and rub his penis between my legs until he ejaculated. Afterwards, he would wipe the semen off me and I would get up and go play. No one ever told me this act was wrong. I didn't know that no one was supposed to go under my clothes or touch me sexually. So naturally, I thought this was normal. That is why it is so important to talk to your children about their personal space and how no one should evade it or touch them in certain types of ways. This went on for about a year or so and then we moved.

There came a time of separation from my dad's family. We began living with his girlfriend who had three children along with her Grandmom and Great-Grandmom in an apartment on 63rd street. I can remember it so well because it was the projects; large low-income buildings filled with low-income families. My siblings slept with the boys and I slept on the couch because the great grand, the grand and daughter had the other bedroom. All the bedrooms were tied up which left me with nowhere to sleep but the living room couch. In this era of my flight, the Chicago Blizzard of 1967 hit. You talk about snow! Man, I had never seen anything like it! The city was at a standstill. Snowbanks were so high that public transportation couldn't move and the city was shut completely down.

The following year, 1968, a tragedy hit the city, the announcement of Martin Luther King Jr's assassination. I saw the results, too. 63rd Street burned down! A time before that event occurred, I remember a grocery store called Red Rooster that took S&H green stamps; you could put them in a book and redeem them for things. (For those who lived in that era, I just took you down memory lane, lol). By now, we were in school and I was attending John Foster Dulles Public School. My dad was working for a potato chip company, delivering bags of chips to different locations and filling their vending machines.

Both my grandfathers passed away in the month of December that year. These events were very dark and scary in my life.

We went to my dad father's funeral in his hometown of Bluefield, West Virginia. At that time, my Grandfather was affiliated with an organization that is still very well known today. During the service, some of the men in the organization carried out a large stainless steel axe wrapped in a pure white cloth. I had no clue of its purpose but when it fell out of their hands and hit the floor, it was the scariest scene I had ever witnessed!

MR. B

While at the funeral, the devil's trap for my life reoccurs: child molestation. This was where my dad, Mr. B, began the first stage of his secret. It started at the funeral, where it was not uncommon for it to be held in people's homes back then. It happened when I slept in the bed with Mr. B and his penis was erected up against my butt. By this time, I didn't say anything because I thought this was a normal behavior. I was ten years old. I wonder why it started after Granddad died? I wonder if it was because Mr. B felt freedom from his own fears of what his dad might have done to discipline him for what he was doing to me.

Living in the projects was an experience that allowed me some interesting memories. I remember playing by abandoned cars, being creative. (Children don't have a clue about that these days, lol, with all these electronic devices…lol). Well, one day while climbing the cars to get to the fence, I slipped, fell, and ripped the back of my thigh. It was the way I fell that caused so much damage. It took years for that scar to leave. I remember coming into the building when the elevator wasn't working. We would have to take these dark stairs all the way up to our apartment. Climbing the stairwell took forever and it smelled like urine. I would try to hurry up and get to our floor! My…what memories.

I moved a lot in my life, not just physically but mentally, as well. Soon, another flight took place in my life. We moved back to 57th and Aberdeen. This building had turned into a family building, too. At this time, there were even more of us living there. Remember, the apartment only had three bedrooms? We were all living on the second floor, again but there was a new addition. Don't ask how my youngest uncle and oldest uncle with his girlfriend and a newborn by another woman, plus my grandmother, my dad and all three of us lived there but it happened. We moved there after the funeral.

I recall how, the block seemed liked family. Everyone knew each other by name and knew each other's children. Back then, the Englewood Community in the City of Chicago was just turning into an all-black neighborhood. The city was segregated. Whites were moving out and we were moving in. Owning a home or building back then was big time. The block club parties were off the chain and neighbors looked out for one another. Talk about a village raising a child.

My family had a black Labrador Shepard mix named Rocky who wasn't afraid of nothing but thunder and lighting. He was jet black with green eyes. He did some crazy things like jump out of the second floor window. He was nuts for real (lol)! Man, didn't the Mailman catch the blues doing his job!

By now, my Uncle, Mr. A, went to the Army and came back crazy as all out doors. One day, after returning from the Vietnam

War, he hid behind a tree with his gun while the children were outside playing. All of a sudden, he started shooting in the air and we scattered everywhere. Later, we found out his brain cells were affected by a chemical called *Agent Orange* that they sprayed on crops over there. All of us kids on the block just thought he was straight nuts for nothing. As I reflect, the bible tells us that *vengeance is mine says the Lord* (Romans 12:19). Still today, I believe this was God's way of chastening him for molesting me.

As I started getting older, I began asking questions about my mom. My heart started yearning for her. A piece of me was missing and I was starting to feel disconnected from life. I wanted my mom. So, I went to my grandmother and asked where my mom was? The replies were, "She's dead," or "She didn't want you all anymore." Those replies were like a knife cutting my soul. I felt so alone. I hurt so bad and cried myself to sleep many nights. Something on the inside of me would not allow me to believe what I was hearing. After a time, I was told to stop asking questions regarding her.

Years later, I found out my grandma was adopted and I believe those were the same questions she asked about her mother, too. I wonder if she received the same responses. I do not know much about my grandma's childhood but that's just a thought that makes you wonder.

My grandmother made the best homemade rolls. Sometimes I would stay up all night trying to see how she made them but regrettably, it never happened. Grandma did not share her recipe with anyone.

Those rolls bring back some interesting memories. There was this time we had a Christmas that was so cool. We all got bikes. We couldn't wait until Spring came so we could ride them. When the time came, we all went outside to ride. Some little boy came up and asked could he have a ride. I said yes and never saw my bike again. I went home crying about the situation only to get yelled at for allowing a stranger to ride it in the first place. Anyway, my dad and uncle went looking for the bike with no success.

MR. C

My oldest uncle was an alcoholic. His drink was Christians Brothers Brandy. I wonder if they are still in business. I watched my uncle tear up a many of Cadillac cars in his time. Drinking and driving was his specialty. His live-in girlfriend and my grandmother were at his rescue, constantly. I watched him deteriorate from self-destruction. This uncle, as well, wanted to have an adolescent affair. There came a time where he tried to kiss me intimately in the hallway of the family building between floors but I was able to push him off me and walk down the stairs. This was the Mr. C in my life. By 1983, my uncle passed away from complications of drinking after falling off the porch while drunk.

Soon another shift took place in my life. This was an era that a child should not enter but it happens. My Dad, two brothers and I moved to 73rd in Yates. I was eleven years old and excited that I had my own bedroom. We had left Englewood and moved on the Eastside to the South Shore area. We thought we were "moving on up" like the Jefferson's sitcom….lol. Dad purchased a two flat building, we lived on the first floor and the second floor was rented out. It also had a basement. I only remember the first set of tenants there. They were foreigners. Our apartment was a two bedroom with a living room, formal dining room, front sunroom, kitchen, and enclosed back porch. It was very spacious. We had a big backyard and a two-car garage.

Now my responsibilities (back then, they were called chores…lol) were to clean the vestibule that separated the two apartments, dishes, laundry, cleaning, cooking, plus emptying the garbage and walking the dog. Anyhow, my brothers didn't do anything but walk the dog and empty the garbage. Ugh is what I still say today…lol. There was the good and the bad. Dad moved an older woman in for a while. I remember how, at one point of her stay, her womb fell out of position and she was in bed for days. After that, I don't recall any other woman living there.

Starting the fifth grade was the pits for me. I didn't have many clothes. To be honest with you, I had five outfits and remember them to this day. There was a great rotation going on. (That's why today God allows me to be blessed with so many clothes that I have to give some away.)

"My God shall supply all your needs." (Philippians 4:19)

"The Lord is my Shepherd and I shall not want." (Psalms 23:1)

Don't ever think Jesus won't take care of you because He will. I remember how I would get beat up a lot at school. That year was a living hell for me.

"Don't provoke your children." (Ephesians 6:4)

My dad was going through a lot of frustration and we, my brothers and I, caught it big time. Dad lost his job, bill payments weren't being met and the mortgage was due. We would get beat with a wide strap that would leave bruises and whelps. I didn't like to take gym because I was embarrassed by what was shown, so I would lie about the marks. I even lied and said I had a brain tumor so I wouldn't have to take gym. I also got the love and attention I was looking for and missing from my mom.

This class bully constantly picked on me. I had a pink dress in the rotation line up and she broke a pen and smeared ink all over the dress. When I went home, I got my butt kicked because I didn't fight her for messing up my dress. I was getting beat up at school and at home. I had no rest and no peace. (I truly had the Spirit of fear when it came to fighting). Dad came up to the school but it didn't make too much of a difference. The following year I was transferred from Bryn Marr Elementary to Myra Bradwell Elementary.

Junior High Years

Now I have entered the six grade. Despite my dad being crazy, I began to get devious. Most would like to know, "Why would you begin to get in trouble knowing the consequences?"

When a house is full of disobedience, the children will follow suite. I began to hang out with the wrong crowd so I could fit in. This was an era of my life when I wanted boys to notice me. I started trying to smoke cigarettes. I was kissing the boys and wearing mascara but that didn't last long. My dad started coming up to the school and getting tight with the teachers so that stopped a whole lot of stuff. Parents today need to interject like that.

My objective of school was changing. Dad was there a lot. In seventh grade, I remember how my right hand was slammed in the classroom door and blood clots were on all of my fingers. This was an attack from the enemy called *physical abuse*. I wasn't bothering anybody but this boy just came and slammed the door on my hand on purpose. He was such a troublemaker! I was at Cook County Hospital all night. My dad made me go to school the next day. Luckily, the teachers allowed me to sleep in class.

I loved to go to summer school because there wasn't much of anything else to do. I would go and get involved in a lot of activities, which consisted of plays, drama classes, etc. to keep busy. During the summer months, Dad would take us to the Drive-In movies in his Cutlass. Sometimes we would ask if he could stop and take us to McDonald's to get something to eat. When he didn't have any money, he would play a game with us and say that if he had to stop the car, he would get us something but you know that the car never stopped, right? Lol.

At this point, the secret in my life was happening often. This was a time when my dad, Mr. B, was beginning to come in my room and have oral sex with me and I had to masturbate him until he ejaculated. This went on until the eighth grade. This behavior spilled over to my brother. I tried to repeat the act on him but nothing happened, so it was a one-time affair. It's hard to say or even think about this but I had become a molester through learned and uncorrected behavior. This is how generational curses begin or continue. These are the roots of problems that you have you to go back to in order to forgive and ask for forgiveness, from yourself and others, to be released and set free. Oh, Glory! That is a shout right there.

Seventh grade was also a year when I would like to run my mouth a lot in class. (Didn't know I was being prepared to be a preacher...lol). I would get caught a lot, which meant notices were sent home and my butt would get kicked. Eventually, I came up with a strategy. I got my dad's penmanship down to a tee and forged his signature. I would copy it if I got a bad grade. Now I don't suggest anyone do this and I eventually got caught. Even though I signed all those letter, I hadn't stopped running my mouth in class. My dad made a pop up visit one day, my teacher

IN THE BEGINNING

addressed this issue with him, and that was all she wrote. I got the hell beat out of me.

As eighth grade approached, Dad started going back and forth to jail. See, Dad made some wrong decisions that led him into a life of crime and left us in the house by ourselves. I learned how to write checks and pay a few simple bills like the lights, gas and a clothing store called Bonds. One time the heat was cut off, Dad was locked up, and we were cold with nowhere to go. Imagine three kids and a dog locked up in our own world, crying out and no one listening. Philippines 4:19 says, "I can do all things through Christ that strengthens me."

Even though we didn't know God, He knew us and helped me and my siblings survive. He had extended His grace to us. Our lives seemed like a living hell but *in the mist of the storm*, Psalms 23:4. (Go get your bible to read the scripture for yourself). Although we didn't understand what was going on, God was with us. You talk about the Grace of God!

Dad would go to jail, get out, and come home and try to get things back in order until the next episode. Then the police would come and kick the door in to get him, again. We were transferred, back and forth, to the family building on Aberdeen. For the most part, we would fend for ourselves.

Dad began to socialize with my teachers more, one male teacher in particular. There were many business transactions going on between them at the time. I don't know what the business meetings were about but they were frequent. Dad was trying to start his own business in photography, which was a slow process and caused him to get involved in other things.

Then, Dad got on the PTA committee and they had a splash party at McCormick Place. Boy, the parents were excited! I can remember it like it was yesterday. By the time everything was over, that party was the talk of the town.

As I reflect just a little, I remember having a dollhouse and my brothers having army figures. They got mad at me and stomped the roof of my dollhouse in. Well, I politely took their army figures and broke them into pieces. I also remember the Susie Home Baker oven and the very first set of muffins I ever made; my brothers played baseball with them! Those memories still make me laugh! My brothers and I fought a lot but we loved each other deeply.

When we started the eighth grade, Dad gave a timeframe to get home from school. We would get out of school at 3:15pm and have to be home by 3:30pm. I only had 15-minutes to get from 77th and Exchange to 73rd and Yates? That was a lot of ground to cover. It seemed impossible but I got it done. It was to keep me from getting into trouble with the boys and so he would know where we were at all times.

During this time in my life, my brothers and I would go to Jewel Food Store and carry groceries to people cars for change. That was our way of contributing to the house financially because dad lost his job and that was our means of eating. At the ages of

IN THE BEGINNING

12, 11, and 9, we had adult responsibilities. At that age we should have been allowed to be just children.

I know earlier in the book I wrote about the gas and lights being out, it was an ongoing situation with us. What was so funny about it was how Dad rigged the basement storage lockers with his camera lighting equipment to project heat so we could stay warm. He may have done some dumb things but he did some clever ones, as well (lol).

As time progressed, I started my menstrual cycle and it seemed like it was the most horrible thing in my life. I knew about it from Sex Education in class but for it to actually happen was terrifying. I had the pleasure of getting my own sanitary pads at the age of thirteen. I was miserable because it kept me sick and the whole nine yards. With all this going on in my life, I still yearned for my mother no matter what they said. I spent many nights crying because I wanted her. The need to have her to hold me and tell me that everything would be all right was very strong. I used to desire that one day we could all live in the same house together as a family. However, that was only a desire.

As my 8th grade graduation approached, my yearning for my mom became greater. I told my dad that I wanted my mom, again but he claimed he didn't know where she was. Then, one day while I was out at the store, a woman approached me and said she knew my mom and me. She gave me a phone number, so I ran home and let my dad know. (The Lord will not allow you to be ignorant of Satan's devices).

Eventually, I got defiant with him and I threatened that if my mom didn't come to my event, I wasn't marching across stage. There wasn't any arguing on that day. I'm surprised Dad got in touch with the lady, who he knew personally, and my mom was at my graduation. It was the happiest day of my life. She bought my graduation clothes and everything. I looked like a beautiful young woman that day; how a 13-year-old was supposed to look. I had brand new clothes with matching shoes. Boy did God make all things new! When she came and got me for the festivities, all we did was cry. She was beautiful. Our conversations on that day didn't consist of why she was never around. We really focused on the right now moment. This was the beginning of what Jesus calls Restoration.

What Satan meant for evil, God was working out for my good. (No matter what the Devil is trying to do to destroy things in your life, when it comes to restoring love, in God's timing, it will happen). We didn't stay in touch right off because my dad had full control and we weren't allowed to see her often. So many lies were told to us children. So much deception and mental manipulation had happened to us. See, there were the lies about her being dead and her not wanting us. It felt so good to be able to hug her. What I had longed for had finally happened. I just wanted to hug my mom. It was like a dream come true.

High School Years

The summer between grammar and high was no different than average kids hanging around outside after doing their chores; going to the beach, and such.

Reflecting back on my eighth grade graduation, when I went on our trip to Springfield, I thought I was doing something great. I had my first passionate kiss with a boy in front of the whole class on the school bus. He was the ugliest boy in our class and the whole class was shouting, OWAH!!!! Boy did it feel good. Yes, I was teased but it didn't matter, he was the first boy that paid real attention to me. After graduation was over, I never saw him again. My esteem was so low; I didn't realize that I only did that because I needed validation.

As the summer progressed, the police were still coming and knocking down the door. In his "cleverness", my Dad purchased a device that allowed us to know when they were coming. That finally stopped them from kicking in the door and we were able to open it, instead. Dad involved us in some of his schemes; we were the lookout crew for the situation at hand. We had to do the scheduling of the shifts of who did what and report it back to Dad. No, Dad wasn't the drug man but he was something else, literally.

In the Fall, my Freshman year started at South Shore High School. Wow.....what a place to be! The school was huge and it was so different than grammar school. I was astounded at the size of the buildings and how many teachers and students were there.

The structure of the classes was different to me. Transferring from class to class was something and the older students blew my mind. I even had the privilege of meeting a student who was twenty-years-old and still a senior. At that time, you could stay in public school until you were twenty-one and then, the system was forced to pass you. I think he was waiting on his turn.

I was more mature physically and dad began making even more visits to my room at night. I even recall finding myself masturbating because of the feeling I would receive in doing so. One time Dad called me but I didn't respond because I was in my room masturbating. When he asked me what was I doing and I told him, he didn't say anything. There I was, at the age of 14, desiring to be sexually fulfilled. This trap from the enemy began to feel good to me.

The spirit of perversion had entered and I was robbed of knowing what it meant to live sacred and holy before God. This was not the way that God would want His daughters to be loved.

Teen years are for enjoying; hanging out with your peers, enjoying school and maturing with life not being sexually entangled. So, if you're reading this book and you are a teen that is sexually active in any shape, form or fashion: STOP! Sex is a covenant God made between a man and woman for marriage. It is designed for intimacy with one another and for the production of mankind. Enjoy your teen years and do not let sex cheat you out of a real good time.

South Shore High had a lot of compassionate teachers and counselors there. September of 1972 marked the beginning of my freshman year. My music teacher was the bomb. She was the sweetest teacher I ever knew. She had so much love for her students. Then there was a man there by the name of Mr. Jones. (In all actuality, I can't remember his name, just his position…lol). He was the Disciplinarian. Whenever anyone would cut class, he was on it. That man would chase me a many of days because I began to get rebellious in school by cutting class. I believe this stage of my life had started because, as most teens do, I was beginning to "smell myself". However, if you think about it, with everything I had already been through, I should have been able to do whatever but not so. Cutting school is not the cool thing to do. Please do not think because you're reading about what I did in my youth in this book that I condone it because I don't. Education is the only thing that is going to get you where you need to be. So, stay in school!

This cutting class season started after being there for a semester. As usual, my last class ended at 3:15pm. Even in high school, I had 15 minutes to be in the house. So, I had to make it in the door by 3:30pm. Sometimes I would actually make it. The school was located on 76th and Constance. Boy, I still don't know how I did that but I did. During these school years, the house chores increased, Dad wasn't working but a new change did occur; we started going to church.

At this point in my childhood, I was glad I was attending church. It was a peaceful, relaxing getaway for me. This was the drawing of God. John 12:32 says, "If I be lifted up all men will be drawn to me."

We attended a church located on 73rd and Cottage Grove. The Pastor was a powerful Woman of God and every time I would see her, I would feel the love and warmth from her. Her name was Consuela York and her presence is still prevalent today. She served as a Chaplain at Cook County Jail and her picture is still a monument there. One day, as my siblings, Dad and I were leaving her church, the Woman of God came over to us and started talking to my dad. I remember when she placed her hand on my shoulder and said, "God is going to use you mightily."

I was shocked and scared. I questioned myself, "What in the WORLD is she talking about?"

I didn't know she was speaking prophetically (the mind of God) regarding my life. It sounded good though. I still didn't know who God was although I was going to church. This God business was foreign to me.

Anyway, Dad was taking us there some Sundays and also, to church on 45th and Princeton on Sunday night for their evening broadcast. (Just a side note, I remember when Dad would do a lot of not eating. He told me he was fasting. I also saw a red cloth in his possession. He said it was a contact to God. It didn't make sense to me back then but my inquiring mind wanted to know.) Fasting is when you stop eating food for religious purposes. By depriving your body of food, you open up your spirit to nourishment of the Word and hearing the voice of God.

Going to church was uplifting for me and I looked forward to it because what I desired in life was there and that was Love. If we didn't go to the church on 73rd, I would find another neighborhood church to go to because I didn't want to lose the feeling of love that I encountered. Dad saw how I enjoyed it, so when I would do something that required punishment; he prevented me from going. My heart would just break. By the time I turned 17, church was obsolete. This was another attack from the enemy that was in the making, turning me away from God.

MR. D

Now, back to my first year of high school...I was fourteen when I met the boy of dreams. Oh, my!!!! Handsome, played basketball and I thought he was the bomb. I liked to watch the boys play basketball. "Shoot hoops" is what we use to say back in the day. Watching them was a form of entertainment for me. I wasn't looking for a boyfriend because my brothers told me I was ugly. (This was one of many attacks of low self-esteem taking place). This particular young man started showing me attention and it started the beginning of another chapter in my life.

We began meeting up with each other during school. When Dad wasn't home, I would sneak him into the house. We would sit around and talk, hold hands, and watch TV before Dad would get in. I had the schedule down to the second. I never was caught. We'd start off kissing but when the unbuttoning of my pants would start, I'd tell him that wasn't happening. This went on for a while until the following year.

In 1973, I really began to have strong feelings for him. I finally allowed him to talk me into having sex because I didn't want to lose him. I lost my virginity in the basement of my home. I remember how I bled after he left. Being naïve, I didn't use any protection and this continued for a while.

I thought I was in seventh heaven; I had my first boyfriend who liked me enough for me to give my body to him. I began cutting classes to be with him, to lay up with him because it made him happy and that made me feel special to him. He was my Mr. D.

During this era of the new relationship, Dad lost the house on 73rd and Yates due to foreclosure. After many raids from the police, he also lost the car. I ran away from home because I was tired of what life was taking me through. I left and spent the night in a home where some other children stayed with no supervision. Then I went to a house where another young lady, who was a runaway herself, went. That didn't last long because the woman of the house got in touch with my dad so he could come and get me. I didn't get in trouble because he was trying to find out what was running through my mind. So now, we were moving and my world was shifting, and another journey began.

Soon afterwards, Dad rented a house on 106th and Rhodes. I was crushed because I was losing the boy of my dreams. Then, Dad transfers me from South Shore High to Fenger High School. Yuck!!!! I met two young women there who I'm still friends with to this day. We had some crazy days but before I get into that era, I'll finish this journey. I was able to stay in contact by way of payphone with my boyfriend at South Shore. We were still able to connect because I would cut school to be with him and get back home on time as if I had been at school all day. I was having sex, watching TV and when my hair was braided and I couldn't get it back like it was when I left, I would have his oldest sister to redo it. It's a wonder my grades stayed up to par.

Now the house on Rhodes was infested with roaches. It was terrible how they would crawl up in the bed. I didn't have my own room, so I had to sleep with my dad, Mr. B, and literally fight the roaches off me. We had slowed down going to church because of the move. Many would wonder how he could continue to molest me and still go to church.

It's called, *having a form of godliness and denying the power there of.* (2 Timothy 3:5)

He was just going but no change had occurred because in his heart he had no real desire to.

Dad continued to fondle me from time to time but it would be late at night. Then one day I got caught cutting school and met up with him on the bus. I was so scared of him, I ran off the bus. It still didn't stop him from beating the crap out of me. Now what's so amazing is that he still disciplined me although he was having oral sex with me and having me masturbate him. Even though what he was doing was wrong, I still had to obey my father on the other issues. He was my parent.

Honor thy mother and thy Father and thy days shall be long. (Exodus 20:12)

Now, I am not saying that any girl should be obedient to sexual abuse; I would encourage that young lady to get help.

Anyway, all this still didn't stop me from cutting school to go meet up with my guy, who I was deeply in love with. Then the ultimate happens, I was fifteen years old and getting sick to my stomach. Things were starting to smell funny to me. There was a gas leak in the neighborhood and it kept me sick, constantly. I began to do a lot of vomiting and then it came to me, I'M PREGNANT!!!

Soon, another chapter in my life began. So what did I do? I tried to contact my mom. I had her address, so I wrote her a letter and told her everything. I mailed the letter but it came back. I put the wrong address on it and my dad got a hold of it. He asked me what the letter said but I didn't say anything. So, he opened it and read it.

IN THE BEGINNING

"So you're pregnant? Who's the boy?" he asked.

I told him and gave up the phone number. Dad contacted his mom and set up an appointment to meet with them. We went to their home in the evening, during a weekday. Dad and my boyfriend's mom went into the dining room and talked. They came out and began to give us options. My dad was very adamant that I was not having a baby because I wasn't able to take care of it. He wasn't going to be responsible for another mouth. On the other hand, his mother let me know how she had my boyfriend, Mr. D, at the age of fifteen and although it wasn't an easy task to be a single parent at such a young age, it could be done.

There was a lot of confusion going on, loud talking, decisions being made and no one is considering us. Finally, my boyfriend asked, "What about us? Why has no one asked us anything?"

Now all eyes were on us. My boyfriend took me into the dining room and begged me to have the baby. He was on his knees pleading with me. I was confused; lost. I didn't know what to do but I had my dad in eye view, who was watching my every move. My boyfriend let me know it was our decision not theirs and we could have this baby and make it work. Of course I listened to my dad, not out of obedience but fear and control. I aborted the pregnancy.

Control is a form of witchcraft where a person controls your mind. Now another journey of my life begins.

My dad made an appointment with Cook County Hospital to have an abortion. It was mid-May and a lot was going on in my life. I was scared out of my mind because I didn't know what was going to happen next. I spoke with many counselors at the hospital. With dad going back and forth to court and our living conditions, I was as confused as they came.

Anyway, my dad met a young woman at the clinic, whose niece was having an abortion, as well. We were the same age. This woman became my dad's new girlfriend and an asset in my life. Their relationship became close. She lived on the eastside, the South Shore area of the city, which was cool because that allowed me to see my boyfriend, the love of my life. I began to spend a lot of time over her house. When she came into Dad's life, a lot of the molestation had ceased. (God had made a way of escape for me).

The love of my life had abandoned me. He was walking in unforgiveness. He treated me like crap and even then, I still chased after him in school and kept calling him. The only time I would see him is when he wanted to screw. It didn't matter to me, as long as, I got the chance to see him. (Low self-esteem will do that along with the fact that I was dealing with rejection). I didn't see him often and only on his terms. That is how the relationship ended up after the abortion.

MR. E

I was out in the "Hundreds" as we called it back in the day and at Fenger High. My new crew did everything together and when I say we did everything, I mean everything. They were the ones who introduced me to Mr. E. We would cut school to go and hang out, meet up with our boyfriends and have sex, go to the show and everything. It's a wonder that any of us passed any classes. Well, I just told on us, so if their families didn't know then, they know now. Mr. E didn't last long. This rebellion came because I didn't care anymore, so I was just out there. Oh but God had a plan, I just didn't see it!

Teens *make your body a living sacrifice, holy and acceptable to God, which is your reasonable service.* (Romans 12:1)

There is nothing cool about group sex and belittling yourself. I didn't know it at the time. We were just doing what we felt was right in our minds.

I was sixteen-years-old, smoking squares (cigarettes for those who don't know) and smoking weed (marijuana), as well. Now I'm not saying that this was a good look because it was not. Don't think I'm glorifying the devil but only stating the foolish mistakes I was making, the wrong turns that were leading to destruction.

MR. F

I met this nice boy on the block and he was a pretty cool dude. He was tall, dark and handsome. Afros were in style and his was huge. Everyone called him by his middle name. He was my Mr. F. We would hold hands and kiss. Even though I was having sex with Mr. F, my heart was still with the one I got pregnant by, Mr. D. I didn't stay at Fenger High for long. Gearing towards my third year of high school, Dad was preparing to go to the penitentiary, so our possessions were going back to Aberdeen. Dad was sentenced and another journey started in my life.

While he was locked up, my mom had an opportunity to get us back. She could've had her three children back! However, her life was her own now and we weren't a part of that equation. This is where the spirit of rejection and abandonment entered in and took root.

By this time, my two siblings and I ended up living with my dad's girl on Ridgeland Avenue with her five kids. Dad didn't know her long at all but he trusted her to keep us while he was locked up. It was something; talk about freedom. I could do what I wanted to do, as long as, I abided by the house rules and went to school. I was still hooking up with Mr. D while staying in contact with Mr. E who I met in the hundreds.

I became very close with my Dad's girl. She kept me by her side. I was close to 17-years-old and learned a lot about maturity from her. She began to school me about life with her own experiences. My brothers didn't stay there long; they went back to the family building on Aberdeen. However, I stayed there for a year. Even today, I still remember my Christmas there. I got a lot of clothes, which is a girl's dream. I didn't have many outfits so to get all that I received that year was off the chain for me and you couldn't tell me nothing! One of the pieces was a mint green skirt with a plaid top and some tan boots with black stockings. That is the greatest Christmas I remember during that dark, cold time. However, as I reflect, it was a form of God's love being shown. Jesus will show up in the mist of dark places.

Anyway, back to my junior year. I began to smoke more and started drinking on weekends and holidays. I was grown-up with and without supervision. My Dad's girl had a pool table that folded, so on the weekend, it was unfolded so we could party. That was actually how I became a pool shark. Pool was my favorite past time along with me having my favorite Christmas drink, White Port and Kool-Aid. Anyone raised during that time might remember what I am talking about. I had a ball during those holidays. That particular New Year's Eve took me to a place in life that I never expected to experience.

The devil had a plan but God had another. My dad's ex-girlfriend was at a family function, an altercation took place and shooting broke out. I could have been shot! God said I would live and not die to declare the works of the Lord. Her sister's boyfriend was shot. Both of us took the victim out of the house and drove him to his place. She laid him on the couch while I held a candle near the wound. She took a blade and burned the end of it, had me to pour some Old Grand Dad 180 proof liquor into the wound before she dug into it. The man just passed out. I took the tweezers and pulled the bullet out. Then, she wrapped the wound and we left him sleeping on the couch. What an experience that was. The Good Lord, Jesus, had angels of protection around me when I didn't even know it. (Be careful out here being in the wrong places because death has no name.) We went home and I had to have another drink before I went to sleep. Nothing else was ever said about the matter. I wonder if he is still alive. I never heard from or saw him, again.

I was really enjoying the company of my boyfriend, Mr. D. I was seeing him more because I was in the area and he could visit with no restrictions. That meant that we could have sex more frequently. (This is actually called a *soul tie* because it didn't matter how many guys I had slept with, I always came back to him.)

As time passed, my dad's girl met another guy. Before long, their relationship progressed and our relationship began to fade. Right before that transition took place, her oldest daughter and I had gotten close, to the point that she knew I was leaving and wanted to leave with me. We had a tight bond. It reminds me of the story of David and Johnathan in the bible found in 1 Samuel 20. Unfortunately, it didn't end that way. Our friendship and love were separated. Her youngest sister started being disrespectful towards me because she was "smelling herself" and we had an altercation. We ended up in a rumble and she got a hold to a pair of scissors and stabbed me in my left eyebrow. As a result, I beat her up pretty bad. Of course, I had to move out but that was just the icing on the cake for me and there started another journey in my life.

I moved back on Aberdeen. Moved in with no explanations of why I was there, just popped up and there I was with my two brothers. I was seventeen and about to go into my senior year. We were living on the first floor and my extended family members lived on the second floor. My dad was serving a little over a year by this time. (In regards to the survival of my brothers and me, it was every man for himself. I can't even tell you how we were living or even getting back and forth to school or eating; only God knows.) Jesus was truly with us. Even though we didn't know Him, He knew us.

When the summer started, I got involved in the marching band through our block club. We had some good times. God will bring joy in the mist of sorrow. There were lots of kids on the block and we were like family. With everything going on with the transition of me moving back to the family building, I lost contact with my boyfriend, Mr. D.

MR. G

This particular summer was exciting for me. I rehearsed often with the marching band and it was a great outlet for me. What's amazing is I can't remember who was in charge of the band. Astounding! One day, we had a marching band event on State

Street by Jones Commercial Business School. That was a school for girls only who wanted to study secretarial and business courses. It would lead them into their field. Well after the event was over, me and my friends from band went across the street and met two nice looking fellas underneath a building. They were actually FINE...lol. Both of us were just melting. Wobbly knees, sweaty hands, the whole nine yards. We couldn't believe they were interested in us. We all began to chitchat. In other words, they were getting their "mack on" and we gave them our phone numbers. Then the one that was talking to me leaned down and kissed me. I was blown away. Here begins another journey in my life.

Mr. G is what I will call him. He and I were inseparable. Morning, noon and night, we were together. I can actually say I was in love. By this time, the young man who I was pregnant by, Mr. D, had graduated from South Shore High school and was no longer a part of my life. I was wrapped around Mr. G. When I brought him on the block where I lived the girls went crazy asking, "Who is that fine black man there?"

The summer had ended and it was time for me to return to school. How I managed to get back and forth to school, only God knows. After meeting his mom, who didn't take no mess, his younger siblings and an one older as well, I was over his house every day, after school.

IN THE BEGINNING

I did a lot of walking during that time of my life. Most of the time I would have fare for the bus just to get back and forth to 74th Street So I would walk from 74th to 57th and Aberdeen, daily. One day while I was on the bus, I happened to look out the window and I saw my mother. She was a crossing guard for the city of Chicago. I jumped off the bus and embraced her because I hadn't seen her in a while. I talked with her until she finished crossing her kids. (The question was asked about how I felt about my mom not intervening in my life. My answer is simply this: Even at a young age, I loved my mother so much that just being able to connect with her was good enough for me). Yes, the feeling of rejection was there but I still yearned for her.

Continuing the story, I would get carfare from her and off I would run to Mr. G's house. Sometime, I would stay there all night and leave from there to school. It didn't matter because I didn't have clothes, only a couple of jeans and tops for the most part.

As time progressed, Mr. G began to take me out with his older siblings. This was my first experience of going to a club, lounge or whatever you want to call it. Both places we frequented still exist today. Here is another journey about to begin. At 17-years-old, who would have ever thought I would be in a lounge. Guess what, else! He was a year younger than I was. We were getting in with no problems. His height played a big part in his maturity. We were at the lounge every weekend or at his house having a drink and playing cards. (My card playing days started with my first boyfriend. That is how I learned the card game Bid Wiz).

There were nights that I couldn't stay at his house so I would have to walk from Marquette and Loomis (which is 67th St) to 57th and Aberdeen by myself. Yes, some nights he would walk me home but either way didn't matter because in a few hours Mr. G would be back in my presence.

Mr. G and I grew closer. I should have been on birth control but I was naïve. In the month of April, I began feeling a little sick during the day but didn't think much of it. By the time May of 1976 came, I missed my cycle and I was pregnant. What was I going to do now? This wasn't in the plan. I had two more months before my senior year was over. I was already struggling to get back and forth to school. I already didn't have clothes to wear and now a BABY! What was I going to do? Well, I told my grandma and uncle (Mr. C.) and their response was, "Get Out!"

They felt I was a bad influence to my cousin who was 10-years-old. When I told Mr. G, he was angry. And there begins another journey in my life.

Dad was still incarcerated when my shift occurred. I moved on Marquette. This was Mr. G's house. Some would ask why I didn't move to my mom's house but I didn't think about that, so I didn't ask.

The bible says, *I (meaning God) will never leave you nor forsake you.* (Hebrews 13:15)

IN THE BEGINNING

I was proud to be a mom but the pregnancy was ugly. I wanted to be a mom to a child that I didn't have. I still had to finish high school, I was out growing the clothes that I had and I stayed sick a lot during this pregnancy, which kept me crying. We went to an OB doctor on 47th and State Street who was the coolest ever. He understood me. I told the doctor how I was staying sick a lot and he prescribed a medication for me that I thought was heaven. I didn't have any more morning, afternoon and evening sickness.

It was getting close to graduation and prom. I was a good three months into my pregnancy and was going into a period of depression. My Mom didn't know about the baby and my pregnancy hid well at that time.

I wanted to quit school, so I went to my school counselor and explained my dilemma. She had me to speak with the Principle of the school. They placed me into a program that allowed me to work and get paid at the school during my free periods and lunch. It was a CEDA program. I'm still grateful today about the program. It allowed me to stay in school and finish. God was making a way even in the wilderness.

Mom bought everything: prom and graduation clothes. I was the sharpest girl there. The dress was beautiful; it was peach with a jacket that had a white lace opening in the back. The dress had spaghetti straps and matching accessories, white shoes and a small white handbag. I was simply elegant as most of the neighborhood stated. The earned income that I received helped Mr. G get his tuxedo to go to the prom with me. This was the first time I ever had my eyebrows arched. I felt special during my prom and graduation experience. As graduation approached, I wrote the correctional facility to try to have my dad released to attend my graduation but he wasn't. You would think I would want him to stay behind bars but in the mist of the turmoil, I still looked at him as being my dad.

After I graduated from high school, I did not get much support. I was shifted from house to house among Mr. G's family. I left his mom's only to live with his sister. At this point, Mr. G stopped coming around and I felt abandoned. When I moved back to his mom's house, I helped with the three smaller siblings and it was peaceful there. I became very close to his mom. We did many simple things together but what was most important is she showed motherly love towards me and that was what I desired. I needed love.

She became my best friend and we talked about everything. We would go and play bingo and she would give me money to play. I would even win from time to time. Sometimes, we would sneak off and go to the neighborhood bar. (And yes, I did have a cocktail here and there in my pregnancy. I know I'm probably being judged right now but I didn't know any better.) This was a way for me, I thought, to break away and release the everyday pressures of life. (Surely, this isn't the way for pregnant women to release, so don't go out there drinking and clubbing because what I was doing was wrong.) Many birth defects could have come with that but thank God; Jesus spared me from my negligence. He truly takes care of babies and fools such as I. Wow…I miss her even today.

Well, my pregnancy was in full bloom and September had arrived. My dad was released from the correctional facility and came to get me from Mr. G's house. Another journey began to take place in my life.

Chapter Two

Moving On...

Adulthood

By age 18, I moved back home with my two siblings. We were all glad to see Dad back at home but nothing had changed in his life. Rules and regulations were laid down immediately. Mr. G was not allowed to come near his house that I lived in nor did he want him in my life. Mr. G attempted to see me a couple of times, however, my Dad was so rude he stopped coming around altogether. I was living in his house and I had to abide to by his rules. I was afraid of my father and he was mentally controlling. I did not know how to get out from under him.

My daughter was born the following year in January of 1977. Without telling the exact day, I'll just say she was a New Year's Baby. What a beautiful child she was. I went into labor on that Thursday of the New Year. My uncle, Mr. A, was the one who rushed me to the hospital that I was assigned to. I was in labor for quite a while but by the time midnight came, the labor became intense and I delivered by 12:15a.m. I didn't actually know what time I delivered because I had passed out from the pain. When I came to, it was 12:45 a.m. I tried to get out of the bed to go to the bathroom and fell and passed out again and when I awoke, I was in a pool of blood. A nurse walking by saw me on the floor and called for help.

My blood type is B-negative which means I am an RH factor and I am to have a RhoGam shot after having a baby, an abortion or losing a large quantity of blood. If I don't, I could die due to my white corpuscles. They can override my red ones and if that ever happens, I'd be in a lot of trouble. That is why I was so weak because the process had begun to take effect. After a couple of hours of rest, I was able to see my daughter.

I was very new at being a mother, so when they brought her to me with a bottle, I had not a clue of what to do. I fed her until the bottle was almost empty. She vomited all over me. I didn't know you had to burp a baby and or even how to do it. They showed me how to do it, though. (Unmarried mothers are not in the plan of God but He looks after us anyway). People actually married young back in the day and they stayed together, through thick and thin.

After leaving the hospital, I had no means of supporting my daughter. My dad contacted my old friend from Fenger High School and influenced her to let me use her address so I could receive Public Assistance. During that time, I was getting to know the daughter I brought into the world. It was a trying time for me. I didn't know the first thing about motherhood but I was about to find out.

Dad wasn't really showing me anything because of his anger. Boy did I have many lessons to learn about motherhood. I burned plenty of bottles heating them up every four hours for feeding. Then there was the massive diaper rash. I must have listened to every homemade remedy that was out there. Then there was the washing of clothes in a different soap than what everyone else used.

We had a dog, Prince, who was a German shepherd. He watched over my daughter. He wouldn't let anybody get close to her. You had to go through him first.

There was this one time when I was so tired of not having enough sleep, I literally got out of the bed, gave my daughter to my dad and slept for eight hours. I didn't care about the consequences because I was tired. That was best sleep I had ever gotten.

Then it came time to start feeding her cereal through the milk. I guess my dad felt sorry for me because he was the one who gave me the tip of doing that. It was on and popping after that. She was sleeping more because she was full. Every nipple that she owned was opened wider and I began to sleeping at night. By time she turned six months old, I was feeding her table food. I still remember her eating her first Bar-b-que bone from the neighbor next door. She had grease everywhere, even down in her pamper.

MR. H

After nine months of being home, my dad got me a job working at a donut shop on the north side of the city. Another journey was about to start in my life. This was my first job. Dad was good friends with a neighbor living on the block and she worked there. The shift started at 5am and she would pick me up. The rides lasted for a while. I found a babysitter on the block, too but the entry to her house was dangerous. I had to go through a poorly lit gangway to get to her front door. I was scared on a daily basis.

During my employment there, I began to hang with a group of people who were way out of my league. Chicago Transit Authority was their name. I met plenty of interesting people there. They were a partying group of people, as well. I began going to the clubs they attended. Eventually, I started dating one of the Conductors. He was my Mr. H. He was dating a girl who worked the train line, as well. She was much older than I was. At one point, she confronted me about our relationship. We had an adult conversation and ended up confronting him. He denied that he dated her in front of her face. So, I dated him some time until the shift came in his life. (His lifestyle changed, drastically. He decided he wanted to live his life as a homosexual). Not sure how I missed that one.

It was hard trying to hang out until 11pm then go home and get right back up at 3am to be at work by 5am. I started taking the train because my riding privileges were terminated. That worked out well because I received a few perks because I dated a CTA employee. Dad was taking all of my money from the assistance I received from the government, so the job allowed me to have some kind of money in my pocket.

MR. I

I went and found an apartment on 69th and Peoria. It was a studio and boy was it full of roaches. My dad had to come and use some exterminating stuff used in the fields to kill those bad boys! You would turn the lights out and the wall would be full of them. After he finished exterminating with whatever he had, I did not see not one of those invaders for a while.

I loved my apartment. Dad had gone and got me a security bar for the front door, so you had to have a key to get in and out. The rent was cheap and my aid check covered it, along with getting food stamps (that's what they were called back then) which took care of the food. Any other money I had was extra pocket change.

After getting my place I began hanging out in the same places my daughter's father, Mr. G, would be. It didn't matter to me that he had moved on. I started dating his brother's, girlfriend's brother. This was my Mr. I. We started getting close and before you knew it, he was my live in babysitter. The relationship didn't last long and I couldn't handle seeing my daughter's father hanging out with the woman he was dealing with. The job didn't last long, either. By this time, I started to hang out with the people I met after the job, which caused me to be introduced to bigger and better things (so I thought). I became a Bartender. Another journey began in my life that had no meaning, substance or stability.

The Streets

While hanging out with the crew from the CTA, I was introduced to a neighborhood bar on 51st and Union. Wonder if it still there? I met plenty of people there, to the point where I had a full-time babysitter. She would keep my daughter whenever I needed, except the days I was off work. Well that position only lasted for a little while. My daughter had to be taken to the hospital due to the bumps that popped up all over her body and when I got her there, I found out that she had bed bug bites. Being a parent takes a lot of responsibility, so don't become parents before your time. So, there went the babysitting services. I ended up having a different babysitter nightly from my siblings, to their girlfriends, to the people on the block. I just knew I had to go to work.

Since I was hanging out now with a new crowd of people, I was introduced to something else in my life that was brand new, too; I had gone from smoking weed to doing cocaine. This is what the devil does: He takes you deeper into destruction. Drugs are a form of witchcraft that controls you. That's why our bodies must not be defiled because they belong to God. Another journey was starting in my life.

Ms. Slick & I

Now I'm getting high, not on a regular basis but enough to get me to like it. (Deception right there). I hooked up with a young woman that I became real cool with. She looked white until she opened her mouth, then you knew she was black. Man was she a schemer! I will call her Ms. Slick. She dated the owner of the lounge and before I knew it, I was renting the back apartment. I let my place go on 69th and Peoria go to move there. I didn't take Mr. I with me. My cousin moved in with me for a minute but didn't stay long. For the time that she was there, we were out every night. We would actually leave the kids in the house. One night even through all the music, we heard the kids running down the side of the building and we ducked out the door to catch them and put them back in the bed.

MR. J

After my cousin moved, my lifestyle changed, again. I started hanging with my friend who looked white. Now this could be looked at as either good or bad, so I thought, because the scenario began to change with men, also. Money was being presented before me. I started dealing with a man who couldn't hold his urine at night and pissed on himself in his sleep. This was Mr. J. Ms. Slick pulled me out the neighborhood on 51st and had me venture into other lounges. This is where I was introduced to a club on 69th and Ashland and another journey in my life started.

I'm still living at 51st and Union but no longer working at the bar. My girl, Ms. Slick, had me hooked up in all kinds of stuff. Not only was she the one that introduced me to cocaine but heroin, too. I thank God today that I never became addicted heroin. It was a down drug and I was one that didn't want to miss anything. Once, I mixed it with cocaine, which was called speed balling, but that wasn't for me, either. Ms. Slick and I did many things together like clothes shopping and such. She was the one who also introduced me to the stores I needed to go to, to look "grown", if you will. Later, I had a dream that the building we lived in behind the bar, caught on fire. I took heed and moved back home. About six months later, it did! (God was with me even in my mess. That was my first encounter of the prophetic. For those who don't know, it means God was speaking to me).

My new place of transition and my new work place was on 69th and Ashland. At that time, I thought it was the bomb. I had transitioned further West on 69th Street and the area didn't appear to be crazy. The lounge was beautiful and so was the neighborhood. The scenery reminded me of a mini Las Vegas. It was like "Lights, Camera, and Action", everywhere! See how the devil takes sin and makes it glamorous? Some of the crew I was hanging out with on 51st Street began to follow me but later they stopped because the environment was different. It was a whole new class of people, even the attire was different, and I grew up real fast. It was filled with the "Upper Class" people, the Pimps and Players, and such.

I was no longer playing with boys; I started associating myself with men. They were working class men who were looking for a good time. These Sugar Daddies, Pimps and Players caused my attire to change dramatically. I had this lavender colored dress made from see-through material because that was the style at that time. Believe me, when I say see through, it was exactly that. I was about to walk out the house with nothing and I mean nothing under it and my dad stopped me and told me to either find something to put under it or don't wear it at all. I did find a camisole to wear under it. By this point, I was getting radical and rebellious. My lifestyle was entering into a ring of prostitution.

Soon I was introduced to the manager of the lounge West on 69th St and before I knew it, I had another bartending job. They asked if I had any experience and I stated that I did. Next thing I know, I was hired! It was a faster pace, which was very different from 51st Street, and the lounge stayed opened until 4a.m. I tell you, that scene was filled with people in high places. I was hooked up with people that I would have never thought I would be socializing with in a million years.

Anyway, I didn't use my real name, Karen, as I did on 51st. I needed to have a name that stood out; it had to be fly and different. This was when and where the nickname KC was birthed, a monster in the making. The name, the lounge and the people there introduced me to a whole, new level of the streets. My life became a party seven days a week and getting cocaine was like going to the grocery store. I started using it daily.

Dad wasn't bothering me sexually in this season because he had a girlfriend who was the same age as me. This was another way of escape from my situation, which the Lord provided. I didn't know God but He was sure looking out for me. Dad's new woman and I got an understanding real quick. She approached me one day as if she was my mama and I had to let her know in a language that she understood, "Don't come to me like that. You don't know me and my mama's not dead. You are just my daddy's woman." (I am putting it nicely due to the readers and my maturity in Christ but I'm sure you can read between the lines). What a relief! I, for once, stood up for myself and my dad didn't open his mouth. My mouth was a garbage can and it was nothing "lady like" about it.

I started hanging out with the bartenders and we became like family. Ms. Slick had gone on about her business by that time so the bar was my new home. Four of us became real tight. Me, Ms. Cunning, Ms. Too Short and Ms. Faithful worked the floor. Ms. Cunning was the one who came around when she had time because she was doing her own thing but we all got together quite frequently. Ms. Cunning and Ms. Too Short fell out with each other because of a man, which I agreed with Ms. Too Sort because Ms. Cunning broke the trust issue. She slept with Ms. Too Short's man. Therefore, it became the three of us.

I ended up moving in with Ms. Too Short and we became "two peas in the pod". We did everything together. She had two daughters and a son. Her girls were older so they were our babysitters. We were at the club every day of the week. It was always something going on. My friends on the block thought I was doing it big because of the fancy cars that I was getting in and out of and of course, I had the big head.

MR. K

As time progressed, I began to hang out with the Proprietor's son. Soon, another journey of my life began. This was my Mr. K. It started out with him teasing me about my jewelry. When I first started there, I was pretty much a "Plain Jane". Then I started dressing according to the atmosphere and he was paying attention. By the way, did I mention that he was married? Oops! I found myself connecting with him, consistently. Well, Mr. K and I became an item. He started taking me with him to the places he would visit. I began to engage with his associates outside the family establishment and boy was he hooked up in the drug scene big time. He looked so innocent but he was the devil in disguise. He was what you would call a "middleman" that would connect the transactions. He was doing pretty well for himself. I began going to his house after his wife would leave and go to work. I had no morals but that was me. I was truly doing me. He somewhat slowed me down. He became the only one I was sexually involved with and then I got pregnant. I told my friend that I roomed with and she turned around and told his mom. Talk about betrayal! I wasn't planning to have the baby so I wasn't going to tell him. Well, when he confronted me about it I lied and told him it wasn't his and that ended our relationship. I had the abortion and kept it moving. I'm exposing the devil to prevent you from getting caught up in his schemes of adultery. It can get you hurt or even kill you.

After the heat in the kitchen calmed down, I continued to work at the bar. I messed around and got my finger caught up in the ice crusher. I could have sued but didn't. That incident allowed me to have a job as long as I wanted. It was a smart strategy but it was manipulation.

MR. L

While still living with my roommate, I started dealing with this guy who was a Pimp. He even looked the part: slick hair, jewelry and fancy clothes. We began talking and got close. Then we started dating. The first night that we had sex was the day I ended the relationship. Well, since his profession was being a pimp, he confessed that I was the only woman he didn't want on his payroll. Why I don't know but I thank God I was covered by the Blood of Jesus. God extends grace to the Unbeliever and I know now that I had a lot of it. Since I didn't have a steady guy, I saw who I pleased.

MOVING ON

As time progressed, my roommate and I began to confess we were sisters and her family adopted me as such. We had the best times of our life working at the club, so I thought. Doing what was right in my own eyesight. Ms. Too Short would have after hour breakfasts at her house after work. We would invite the prestigious ones over and cook. I would cook the grits. I still cook a mean pot of grits today, not lumpy. We were the party house. One morning, the Proprietor (the owner and our boss of employment) came with one of our regular customers, which blew our minds. They didn't eat; they were there to get high, drink champagne and such. Our house was known for getting a great breakfast after hours. We were considered the "Middle Men of Destruction". I was engaged in some truly sinful behavior at that time in my life.

MR. M

Well the breakfast scene didn't last too long in that capacity because my roomy began dating a truck driver. So, she slowed down doing her thing but it didn't stop me. I respected her man when he came over. He treated me cool and she didn't have to worry about me sleeping with him because I had respect for her. After their relationship ended both of us started to deal with the DJ's at the establishment. That's when I met my Mr. M. Boy did we act a fool back then! We did everything together including going to dinner and having breakfast after work. All of us became inseparable. Our relationship went on for over a year. Then my relationship with the DJ that I was dealing with came to a halt. I had moved on and he didn't want to let go but it was best for the both of us. We both were looking for love in the wrong place, which was in each other and the void wasn't filled. My roommate and her man stayed in the mix for a while then they split, as well.

One time in our scenario, someone broke into our house. We didn't understand how her things were taken and mine weren't touched. It was unbelievable! My roommate, Ms. Too Short, thought I had something to do with it. We never did understand that move and it took a toll on our relationship. We had been through so much together but soon our friendship began to get shaky. I quit my job at the bar on 69th Street and ended up moving out of my best friend's home. I started working at a club that was on 67th and Ashland that was quiet with no business. I didn't stay there long at all.

Although I left that didn't affect my relationship with Ms. Faithful. In fact, we still talk today. Soon, another journey in my life took a turn.

I moved back home with no job and a baby but I was still running the streets. I was back to finding a babysitter which wasn't hard to do because whoever wanted to watch her could. Terrible I know but that's where my mindset was.

I was still partying at the club on 69th Street and hanging out with the same people there. The younger crew on the block thought I was in the mix during that time in my life. I was still clowning and out just about every night like I was working there. Nevertheless, a shift came because my finances weren't as tight as they were when I was working there, so my lifestyle slowed down. I had to make everything fit within my aid check. With me paying dad, it wasn't much.

I eventually moved into a new place. I started seeing Mr. K, the owner's son, off and on, again. We both knew it wouldn't be the same so it just became something to do with the both of us. He was in it for the sex and I was in it just to say I was with him. (Once you let strongholds go, do not let those demons back in because they come bringing more with them and they are even stronger than before.)

I began bringing others into my madness on 69th Street. My brother and his girlfriend and some others from the block wanted to see where I hung out. When you're on your way to hell, the devil will implement everyone in the journey, including family. Taking them to my hangout with the car traffic, fancy looking people and light setting looking like Vegas blew the mind of his girlfriend. It was a "stepping stone" for her.

Didn't know I was a leader then. As I tried to keep up the image there, I was slowing fading into the background. I stopped going out for a while and took on the responsibility of being a mother. Look where my mindset was. I was going out every now and again. My dad kept in touch with my ex-roommate, Ms. Too Short, and our friendship was reconciled. Dad helped her get a job at the lounge, too. I would go by to visit from time to time but our relationship wasn't the same at that moment. It was something that had to be worked on. We finally came to our old selves, again.

One day while I was out, I ran into my first love, the young man who I used to deal with when I was 15-years-old, Mr. D. My heart skipped a beat as if I was a kid again...soul ties. We talked for a minute and exchanged numbers. Later, I went to a party on the east side of Chicago (South Shore Area) and it was jammed packed. I was sharp with my wine colored pants suit. Anyway, I found him to let him know I was there, had a drink and left. I didn't do house parties so I called it an early night after getting me a pig feet sandwich off the truck. I know many are laughing while asking, who eats that? While others are saying, I remember when....lol!

MR. N

After the party, I didn't hear from him for a minute and I wasn't waiting around for the call, either. I was putting extra funds in my pocket by tricking off with a particular man that I knew. He was Mr. N. My youngest brother was my babysitter so when he stopped watching my daughter that put a stop to that. Ladies your body is worth more than a price you tag on it.

According to the bible, "You are a chosen generation and a royal priesthood." (1Peter 2:9)

MOVING ON

You are better than that. Don't sell yourself for material things. In the bible, there's a story about a woman called Mary Magdalene. Her lifestyle included being a prostitute but when she met Jesus, she then knew who she was in him and never returned to selling her body again.

I finally I got a call from the man who took me back down memory lane, Mr. D. We started back kicking it hard. I would go to his apartment and just lay up. There was a point in our life where I contracted a sexual transmitted disease from him. Out of stupidity, I apologized and said it came from me knowing I was clean. In my mind, I didn't want to lose him but in all actuality, I was wrestling with principalities in high places; powers that I could not fight because I didn't have a relationship with Jesus. He was half working at the time and I wasn't working at all. Sure enough, I got pregnant. This pregnancy was more of a revenge pregnancy. My dad couldn't make me get rid of this pregnancy; I was pregnant for all the wrong reasons. I wasn't looking forward to the change that came between us. Another journey started in my life.

On December 29th, I got the results back from the doctor's office confirming I was pregnant. I was so nervous because I knew it was going to cause friction between my dad and me. Here, I have a 3-year-old and one on the way. Have to start making preparations. I told the father of my child to be that we were pregnant and he told me it was not his. A whore I was but I knew who the father of my child was. We split up. It broke me down because I was thinking that we could be the family that I so desired but...

I was frustrated and didn't know what to do. My dad was like whatever and I felt abandoned. (I wonder why I never had anyone there for me.) Looking for love in all the wrong places or even in the places you thought you could get it, turns in the opposite way. I went over to Ms. Too Short's house and talked with her about it. She was very sympathetic and allowed me to move back in with her.

New Year's Eve of 1979, I decided to go to a party with Ms. Too Short. We were on the south side of Chicago at a little corner bar that was always poppin'. She was also a Bartender there. Afterwards, we left to go to an after hour joint. While sitting there drinking our Mumm's champagne and smoking weed, a shootout began and the whole place got up. I, literally, had to jump behind the bar to keep from being hit. That's how I brought in 1980. I'm still here. Thank you, Jesus! It was only by God's Grace.

As the new year approached, I filed for Section-8, which is a Supplement Housing Program. I knew I had to make a quick decision because I was about to have two children. There I was going on twenty-two years old, pregnant with my second child, trying to survive with the pressures of life from childhood abuse and molestation, to no stability in the home. All of this came because of generational curses from my family. Yet, I was still alive with a very strong and capable mind. It was only by the Grace of God!

When the month of March came, Ms. Too Short, Ms. Faithful and me would always celebrate our birthdays because the dates were so close together. Mine was the 24th, Ms. Too Short's was the 27th and Ms. Faithful's was April 8th. We would party all the way through the month. I didn't allow my pregnancy to stop the flow. So, guess what! It was on and poppin'! I was too careless to even think about the health of the child I was carrying. I was concerned about having a good time. The bible talks about us being lovers of ourselves and that is exactly who I was (2 Timothy 3:2).

That year we had a cake made to look like a penis standing up and everyone agreed that was why I was in the shape I was. They were definitely right. I smoked weed laced with PCP and drank champagne. My dad was the photographer that year and some of those pictures were notorious. What a party! The world will have you deceived.

*For such people are not serving our Lord Jesus Christ but their own appetites. By smooth talk and flattery, they deceive the minds of naïve people. (*Romans 16:18, NIV)

When you:
- are not under the covenant of the ark of safety
- have not accepted Jesus Christ as your Lord and Savior
- haven't received the call of salvation

You are listening to the lies of the devil who is the father of all lies and you are naïve, fulfilling your flesh and being deceived.

To get some finances flowing, I started back pouring whiskey on 51st and Union during the day and I was off on the weekends. I got back in touch with my girl, Ms. Slick. I quickly found out there was a new sheriff in town in the life of the owner and Ms. Slick wasn't calling the shots like that no more. This new girlfriend was a handful. She was much older and had a little game about herself, too.

During my pregnancy, I didn't hang out with my roomy much. She did her thing and I did mine. Although she allowed me to move back in, it just was not the same. Ms. Slick and I would go out from time to time and she would take me over to her man's house, which was on the lakefront. It was beautiful. She was now dating the owner of the neighborhood bar I worked at. So, we would eat and kick it there. She would get her little ends (money) and we would go. Then one day her new boyfriend asked me to come over but I didn't have a clue why. When I got there, he put a large amount of money in my hand and asked me to screw him. I cursed him clean out but kept the money. By this time, I was a good seven months into my pregnancy and it was really time for me to quit the bar scene and I did.

Father in the name of Jesus; let your daughters know that you will provide all their needs according to your riches and glory in Christ Jesus. Let your daughters know that their bodies are temples and that they are uniquely and wonderfully made in Your image (Psalms 139:14). Allow your daughters to know that they are of a royal priesthood and that they are the apple of your eye. I thank you Father, in Jesus Name. Amen.

While staying over Ms. Too Short house, I would walk from 56th and Justine to 57th and Aberdeen to see my family and the folks on the block. I was seven months pregnant and as huge as a house. To make myself feel better I decided to try to dye my hair a blonde color. It turned out to be three different colors. It had the nerves to be cute. The roots were black, the middle blonde and the ends were red. Don't ask me how because to this day I still don't know how I did it.

I got up to 250 pounds in weight during this pregnancy. I couldn't wear shoes because my feet were spread so wide and swollen. I had to wear Dr. Scholl's shoes, the ones with the wooden bottoms. I had gained so much weight that my doctor was going to put me on bed rest. I was miserable.

My mom was moving out of her apartment and gave me her old dining room set. I took it over to Ms. Too Short house and let her have it. She was ecstatic.

I began to circulate around, here and there, still partying because that's all I knew to do. Even though I was going through different seasons of my life, my mindset had not changed. Maturity hadn't totally set in.

MR. O

Let me share something with you here: When you become a parent, it is no longer about you because now it's about the child and you. I hadn't got there yet.

I went to one particular house party and ran into an old friend of mine. He was the nephew of my dad's girlfriend that watched over me while he was locked up. He was fine when we were younger and now he was exceptionally gorgeous. Well, we hooked up and started hanging out and enjoying each other's company. Before you knew it, we had engaged in sexual activities. Yes, I was good and pregnant. I asked him why he wanted to get down like that and his answer was he had never had any pregnant (you can guess what) before. That was a tripped out answer but he made me feel special at the time.

Young Ladies, this is why you must wait on the Lord for your soulmate, your husband, before having sex and having a family. In this process of life, a woman is in a very vulnerable, emotional state and needs to be comforted by her husband. Wait on the Lord, Jesus Christ. That guy is dead and gone but he was my Mr. O.

As it got closer to my due date, I had everything set up at my mom's address, including my mail. When my mercy check (that's what I called my public aid check) came everything was cool but when the papers came talking about it was confirmed that South Chicago Hospital was where I would have the baby, she hit the ceiling! She had no clue I was pregnant. I didn't want her to know that I was on baby number two and not living up to her expectations. See, Mom had this dream of me going to college and being someone big in society. We had this conversation while buying my prom dress coming out of high school. She didn't even know then that I was pregnant with my first child.

By this time, Ms. Too Short and I have had a falling out. I really can't remember what the fight was all about but it was serious enough for me to move out. I had to move back home with my dad. I got my things and left the dining room set there. Out of anger and the influence of my father, I went and got my kitchen table set back. I did it when she was at work and the girls weren't there. When she came home, saw I had been in her house, and took back the kitchen set, she was very mad. Most of you who are reading this book would say I was wrong and call me everything but what my mama named me but that's where I was mentally. You have to be able to confront your past and your part in it before healing can truly take place.

It wasn't too much time after moving in with Dad that my son was born. August of 1980, I was a mom again. I was in a situation that was unbearable. After having my son, my mercy check was due and I had to go to the currency exchange to pick it up. It was hot as the devil outside, one day. I was 22 years old and my dad had me dressed in winter pants, a shirt, a sweater, socks with flip-flops and a winter skullcap. He said that he didn't want me to get sick because my pores were open because I just delivered a baby.

Wonder why the young women today who have children don't have the same concept. I stayed at my Dad's house on Aberdeen for a minute. By the time my son was about 3-4 months old, Dad tried to, literally, have sex with me. He tried to insert his penis within me and I lied and said it hurt. Most would wonder why I didn't try to fight him off me. I was still afraid of my dad. Fear will cause you to do things that you know aren't right. Young people don't let fear stop you from doing what's right in protecting yourself and others. Go tell an adult you trust who can help you or that person. Call 911 or a rape or abuse hotline. God hasn't given us the spirit of fear. If you are afraid, still reach out with all your might.

He, my dad, only stopped because he got frustrated and I was of no use to him. I felt relieved because I didn't have to go through that process any longer. I felt freedom for the first time in my life. There's a scripture I would like to share and it simply says, "Who the Son sets free; is free indeed" (John 8:32). Even though I didn't know Jesus, He knew me and caused my "Red Sea" to be removed. He took a big obstacle out of my path. As my friend, Meochia Nochi Thompson would say, "He conquered my Goliath!"

Soon, a new, complete journey started in my life.

MOVING ON

Chapter Three

The Separation...

After that last unsuccessful encounter with my dad, he spoke with the realtor who was leasing to my grandmother (dad's mom) and got me a one-bedroom apartment on 80th and Commercial. My son was 3-4 months old and my daughter was three and a half. I moved into the apartment with nothing but a kitchen set, bed and I also had a baby bed for my son. I was content because it was mine. This time in my life got very crazy. Most would say, "You're life was already crazy," but this is where life got out of control.

My son was a good child when it came to sleeping. He would go to bed at 10pm and would sleep until 7am in the morning. This schedule started from the time he came home from the hospital. He was a good baby because he slept all night. When it came to feeding him, I couldn't afford Similac so I switched him over to Carnation milk and Karo syrup. When I took him to see the Pediatrician, they would get on me and say, he was too big. I told them I couldn't afford milk, WIC wouldn't accept me as a client, and the doctors weren't any support in helping. Therefore, I did what I had to do. That was that. For a while, I was just there living off my public aid check.

MR. P & MR. Q

My Dad got me a job at another lounge. Before that job, I was still hanging out with the waitress that worked on 69th Street She lived in a family home on 69th and Honore. Even with her relationship, I got caught up with the wrong people and met a man who wanted me to sell drugs for him. In his eyes it didn't work out so he came and got his stash and I never saw him again. God was looking out for me so much. I thought it was a bad thing because I needed the money but it was best for my future that he left. After a while, I stopped hanging with my friend because my dad didn't want me over to her house every weekend. So, I was back in the house. The spirit of control was still over me.

Soon, I start dating a man who was 30 years older than I was. Mr. P is what I'll call him. He was truly a young minded Sugar Daddy. He loved to dance. I made the mistake of allowing him to move in. He was married but I didn't like living alone. I never experienced being married and so I never looked at it as being a terrible thing. He furnished the house and paid the bills. I traveled with him and drove his brand new car but he became a "pain in the butt".

At the beginning of our relationship, I was dating a younger man I'll call Mr. Q, on the side. Mr. Q understood the purpose of Mr. P, so it wasn't a problem for him. After a while, Mr. Q left the scene because he got ill and that eventually took his life.

During the era of Mr. P's stay, I went back to school to try to get a career in the medical field, which was one of my heart's desires. I wanted to follow both my grandmother's, Rudd and Wright, profession in the Nursing field but, unfortunately, I didn't make it. My dad's girlfriend, who was four days older than I was, wrote my paper to get me into the entry exam program at Malcolm

X College where I started this particular journey. I went to school during the day and bartended at night. It didn't last because I didn't have the financial support to keep me there. I decided to quit school and continue working. The relationship ended between Mr. P and me. Then, another journey in my life started.

MR. R

I moved on the east side of town and was looking for work; instead, I met this guy named Mr. R. He was a slick one but he taught me some things in the process of growing up. He taught me the business aspect of running a lounge. I learned how to read between the lines of someone trying to con me for their benefit. He helped me get a job being a bartender on West 79th Street but it didn't last long. His family had a lounge on 79th and Exchange. I would work there for free as a waitress on the weekends because of him. I thought he owned part of the lounge...(Ha, Ha, Ha)! At this time, my self-esteem was very low. He was a very smooth talker and before I knew it, he had me give up my place on 80th and Exchange and we got a place together on 71st and Cornell. That was the most horrible year of my life.

MR. S

During that short time of my stay at that lounge, I formed another relationship with Mr. S. He was my way of escape, mentally. He was someone I met in the lounge I worked at who loved young women. I fit the description of the character that he was looking for and that is why I was sneaking around.

The relationship with Mr. R was an abusive one. I got the crap beat out of me just because I needed a way out. I settled for him and used Mr. S to help me through it. Of course, no amount of comfort in the world can shield you from the harshness of an abusive relationship.

Soon, a way to completely get out of that bad relationship presented itself. We were evicted from the premises and my things were put into storage. We lived with his sister for a hot minute but she told us we had to leave. I never transferred my daughter out of school from the old neighborhood we lived in which was good. I was able to get back into my old neighborhood, only in another building with a different management company. I made it out of the relationship alive and without him in my life.

One night, I went to a party in a lounge that was located on the lakefront of Rainbow Beach. The lounge at that time was for the "elite". Well, I went there not knowing that Mr. R was there and he snuck and followed me to my house and beat the crap out of me for showing up where he was. After that scenario, I never went there again and never saw him again, either.

MR. T

I started looking for a new job and came across one on 79th and Escanaba. It was a little storefront bar with a small cliental.

THE SEPARATION

However, when it came to parties, man, it would be on and poppin'! The owner of the bar was married and had two women on the side, me and the other bartender. He was my Mr. T. He made the other woman the manager, which he stated at the time I should have been. Somehow, he swore up and down I was stealing. There really wasn't anything to steal because no money was really coming in like that. It didn't make any difference to me. Actually, his accusations made it more acceptable to me because I was able to deal with another person I had my eye on. His was on me, too. I would see the owner after hours on occasions and would fix him something to eat and talk to him, as well. He was cheap so I quickly learned what I had to do with him. To be financially paid, I had to ask him for a loan and never return it. I felt that I shouldn't have to because I was sleeping with him. Didn't know my self-worth and didn't know that Jesus looked at me differently.

MR. U

Mr. U was another young man who would flatter me, buy my champagne and take me to the lounges that stayed opened until 4am. He was truly a "Wine Her and Dine Her" with his fine self. We kicked it for as long as I worked at the neighborhood lounge. Also in the equation, I had a play Momma who would come to the bar and drink nothing. She and I would do nothing but talk on the phone about the dirt that would go on in there. She was my sidekick for real. One year I had a birthday party there, which packed the house and I tell you I went to my mom's closet and got a cream-colored dress that was tailor made. It was satin with ruffles that went up the side to the upper thigh and the collar was ruffled, as well. It went into a V-neck cut, which exposed some of my breast. Money was coming from everywhere along with champagne that night. The bar itself made a couple of grand. The Bartender, who was the Manager, had a birthday party after me but it came nowhere near it. I hung out at that lounge for a couple of years until Mr. U took me to a lounge on 80th and Halsted and another journey began in my life.

THE SEPARATION

Chapter Four

Captivity...

CAPTIVITY

The journey that started in this section of my life had me held in captivity for five years. I got caught up and didn't know how to get out. It had its ups and its downs. With it came laughter, tears and troubles. If I could do it over in a different way, I would. Let's get to the journey:

Mr. U took me out to a lounge on 80th and Halsted. It was a club that stayed opened until 4a.m. After going there several times, someone mentioned they needed a bartender. I applied for the position and got the job. My sidekick, Mr. U, left me there and I didn't see him for weeks. When he popped up, there was another woman who took my bartending position at the old location and she became the mother of his child. So now, he was gone. There was a pattern of rejection and abandonment in my life. That type of negativity comes with the lifestyle of wickedness that I was living.

One night I went by the old lounge that I used to work at to have a couple of cocktails. Even though my children were young, I taught my daughter how to use the phone. I would tell her where I would be at in case of an emergency; she knew where to call me. Well this particular night someone called the police on me for child abandonment. My daughter calls and I come to the house and the police were there. I lied and told them I was at work but it didn't matter, I still went to jail. Before I left with the police, I put my bail on top of the refrigerator along with food stamps, called my dad and gave him the scoop and put the dope inside my son's pamper. After my dad made it to my place, they took me to jail. I was working on 80th and Halsted but wasn't really hanging out there like that, so they didn't know what was going on with me. The next night that I was supposed to go to work, I couldn't because I was still in jail. After being bailed out, my kids and I stayed with my dad. I went back to work on Saturday night. My boss knew it wasn't like me to miss work. When I showed him the bail receipt, I kept my job.

MR. V

Now that I was a big girl, I felt like I could do this thang called life here and then came the "Captor" of my life that held me in bondage, once again. We will call him Mr. V.

Mr. V began to show a lot of attention toward me and his bate was money and drugs. He started by getting me high free, without me having to do anything for it. This was a setup for real. I began to see him on a regular basis. Then one day I invited him to my house and that was the first time we had sex. Afterwards he was screaming, "I KNEW IT WAS GOOD!"

Weeks later, he moved in. We paid the bills and he supplied the drugs. I was snorting cocaine for breakfast, lunch and dinner. I stayed high. The devil thought this was my death sentence but God! Then I graduated, I was being elevated in the world of darkness. I went from tooting cocaine to smoking it. Back then, they called it freebasing. Both of my children were of school age and they didn't have a clue of what I was into. I was partying every night on a whole new level and not sleeping for three to four days in a row.

Mr. V was taking me somewhere I had never been nor seen before. The high, I learned later, was a rush that allowed me to think I was someone I was wasn't. This level of getting high took me into new dimensions. Now I'm not glorifying the devil but I want every young woman who reads this book to be careful because the devil will set you up, take you places that look good only to kill you in the end.

The bible says, "He comes to steal, kill and destroy." (John 10:10)

But Jesus! Oh, Glory! Hallelujah…. I'm not dead today!

Now, let's get back to the journey:

I was smoking dope on a regular basis. Now watch how he did it: One night he got mad at me after I came home with a package (cocaine) and asked him to cook it so I could get high. Well he wouldn't do it, so I did it myself. That was the first time that I ever cooked cocaine and it made him mad. Mr. V told me not to ever cook dope, again. I didn't but it never stopped me from smoking because I was always in an atmosphere where I could.

The one bedroom apartment out grew us so I found a place on 72nd and Coles. It was a beautiful third floor apartment. It had two bedrooms, a formal dining room, living room and kitchen. It was right around the corner from my Dad's house. Mr. V was a cab driver. Soon, Mr. V began to show his real colors. He was a woman beater.

See how that abusive spirit followed me?

It started as a child and kept resurfacing. I was caught up in the relationship so bad and I didn't know how to get out. At that time in my life, I don't think I really wanted to get out because of the lifestyle I was living. I honestly felt like I owed him because I was the cause of him losing his primary job. I went to go and get some cocaine while I was high as a kite and wrecked his cab. After that, he lived with me with no income except what I made from the lounge and that wasn't much.

After a couple of years of fighting and living in that nightmare, I didn't know how to get rid of him. Eventually, Mr. V became my live-in baby sitter. I start having relationships with other men while he was in the house and he did the same. I would take the house phone with me so he couldn't call his women on the phone I was paying for. That was so foolish though because what if something would have happened to my kids. (Talk about Jesus watching over fools and kids).

MR. W

With all that in mind, I started dealing with another married man. We will call him Mr. W. HE WAS FINE! He was my showpiece. We would never act like we were kicking it on the job but some did know. He married at a young age and felt like he was missing out on life. Well, I was going to be the person to fulfill his fantasy. We were a hot item and that had Mr. V very upset because he thought he had put enough fear in me not to cheat....NOT! So, he started seeing someone else, too. Now we both doing our own thing and in the same house and it didn't matter to me, as long as he watched the kids.

Mr. W would lie on his friends just to stay out late with me. One night Mr. W and I got a hotel room and stayed until check out time. At this point, I was out of control. I went over to my mom's house and got her old man to bring me home like I had been there all night but Mr. V knew better. As soon as he left, the fight was on. That was the last fight we'd have in the house.

I had a birthday party and Mr. W was excited about it. We took many pictures that night. Many people were asking Mr. V if he was coming. He replied, "I'm not coming to her party with her other man being there."

By now, I didn't give a cuss. The party was the bomb! It wasn't too much longer after when Mr. W lost his job and left the scene. I just went back to cuddling with Mr. V. and we were going to try to make this thing called a relationship work. My kids were ages 8 and 5, both in school, and I'm catching the bus with them, taking them there and picking them up. My daughter got upset with me one day because I wouldn't do what she wanted me to do so they ran away from home to my dad's house around the corner. What's so funny? In all actuality it isn't. I was high, as usual, the whole morning went by, and I didn't know that they weren't in the house. When I noticed, even in my madness, I knew to call my dad and they were there. I went and got them after listening to the long ya da ya da ya da from my dad but I tried to beat the crap out of them because of their disobedience of leaving the house. I began the same pattern my Dad started when I was a child. Although I was in the wrong, they still couldn't get away with anything.

How confusing were my thoughts and behaviors?

Soon, I realized that I had to get a babysitter, so I hooked up with a woman in the building. I paid her thirty dollars for the weekend. One day I sent my daughter to pay her but I was hung over and half sleep so I gave her sixty dollars, instead. By this time, I was teaching my daughter how to count money because I needed a banker and she was the prime candidate. My daughter tried to tell me but she couldn't get through to me. When I came to my senses and realized my money was short, my daughter told me what I had done. The babysitter didn't want to give my money back so I fired her. After that, she ended up moving. She had put the word out that she was scared. I don't know why because I didn't threaten her. I guess it was the company I kept.

MR. X

By now, Mr. V and I found a three bedroom across the street from where we were living and it was huge. The kids had their own bedrooms. After getting the apartment, I was not even concerned about packing. I just moved the things right into the place (ghetto for real).

For the next two years, the relationship between us was cool. We were trying to be a family but things began to turn for the worse. Once again, I drifted off into another relationship, only this time it was with one of the brothers of lounge. We will call him Mr. X.

Now, Mr. X was a smooth talker and a whore from his heart but he was a good-looking one, so that didn't matter to me. I was just another trophy on his shelf but our relationship became real close. I was spending a lot of time with him so I wasn't home a lot. There were so many times that I would be so high off the pipe with him and end up catching a cab home, it wasn't even funny.

One day after being up all night with him and half the day, I went outside and got into this car thinking it was a delivery cab. Come to find out it was just some man who was parked there. He took off with me in the car. I guess he thought he was going to have his way with me because of the condition was in. He drove me into this half-gated community on 79th St by Steward, where there was a small lagoon. I was high but I knew I wasn't supposed to be there. I jumped out of the car while he is driving and ran for my life. Once again, God had His hand on me.

I would see my children during the week but on the weekends, I was in and out. Mr. V was a full time dad to my children but that costed me, too.

Since I started dealing with Mr. X, my finances increased and so I started putting my aid check up, giving it to my daughter, along with my tips. I had an agenda, which was to move without Mr. V. Didn't know when but I knew it was going to happen.

During that season of being at 72nd and Coles, I ran into my daughter's father, Mr. E. He came by the house to see his daughter with his woman but the kids weren't there. They went to visit their cousins. Now I'm smoking dope (cocaine) like crazy and I had the nerve to show her father the tools that Mr. V was using like I'm innocent. Check this out, to show you how stupid I was; don't you know that I could have gone to jail? However, Mr. E never said anything to me and I didn't see him again for years after that.

I was living large but remember I told you that Mr. V watching my kids costed me. He molested my daughter and he physically abused my son. I had no idea. There weren't any marks on his body but Mr. V would slap him around. When it came to my daughter, I found myself back in the judicial system regarding my children. She told one of the counselors at her school and I was able to wiggle my way out by going back to school. I was put on probation for a year to help clean up my act. The cost of my daughter's pain was a nightmare all over again; it was a repeat of all that had happened to me as a child.

MR. Y

By the fifth year, my relationship had totally diminished with Mr. V and my relationship with Mr. X slowed up after a year's time, so I got involved with a new drug dealer. We will call him Mr. Y. He was my way out from Mr. V. I had found a place located on 74th and Coles. My game in the streets with the drug scene had picked up. I'm now running the streets with my best friend who was also a bartender there. We will call her Ms. Too Tall. We were two thieves in a pot together. She also was dealing with one of the brothers there.

Anyway, I got involved with Mr. Y and another journey started in my life.

Now, if you notice, there is a pattern in my life going on.

All of the men are drug dealers or associated with drugs. The drugs were my way of escape to dull the pain that I had never dealt or confronted. The men were the fast life, the money, the glitz and glamor, and love that I looked for because I was trying to look good and be somebody.

Women, teens and young girls, you are valuable in the eyes of Jesus Christ. His love is unconditional and you don't have to sell yourself short or lower your standards of life under any circumstances. Jesus' love is everlasting and because of His love, your life can go beyond the skies.

The bible says in Ephesians 3:20, *"Now unto Him that is able to do exceedingly and abundantly above all that we ask or think."*

The streets, a man nor the world can take you where God wants you to go in life.

CAPTIVITY

Chapter Five

Freedom in the Wrong Way...

Mr. Y. was a well-known drug dealer on the Southside but he was the person that was used to slow me up some while I was out on the streets. I began to sell drugs at a high rate but I did it from the access of phone purchases. That gave me time to be at home more with the children. Mr. Y had access to the apartment because I portrayed myself as being his wife.

Most would ask, "Why would she give this man access to the house after her daughter had just experienced being molested by her previous live in?"

Selfishness and naivety is the best way I can answer that question. Being more concerned about what I wanted than her safety. This was my desire since the age of 17. God's covenant for His children is for them to be protected and safe. I wasn't there, yet.

The downfall of Mr. Y was that he was addicted to another substance called Heroine. I tried watching him try to kick that habit but it was a hurtful thing. I would watch him get clean and help in the process but then he would get right back on it. It didn't stop him from being a businessman in the wrong world though and I had become a part of it.

No, I wasn't the only woman in his life but he made sure I was taken care of. When he came around there would always be a group of men with him, which were his bodyguards. When my kids would ask who they were and I would lie and say, their uncles. I was still working at the lounge on 80th and Halsted during this time.

My relationship with him was different and I began to have feelings for him. I wanted his time because he was producing more than drugs and money. It wasn't about expensive jewelry and fine wine. He was treating the kids well and replacing furniture in the apartment. His affection towards me was different and I wanted to hold on to that feeling but he couldn't produce it on a full time basis. Our relationship became an off and on thing. So, I continued seeing the owner of the lounge when I wanted to and Mr. Y, as well.

The game escalated and I started making drug transactions by way of three-way phone calls. I was doing my thing. I was even teaching my daughter how to count cash by the stacks. I befriended a young woman, which we will address as Neicy. She was my next-door neighbor. We became running buddies. When we went out, we did just that. We pulled all-nighters. She was a little older than I was and from Decatur. She was shacking with an older man, who was a truck driver. She took care of his young daughter.

One night we decided to take a binge and go out. My daughter kept her boyfriend's daughter. We ended up at 80th and Halsted and the games began. We didn't get home until the next day about noon or so. My daughter took her little brother and the baby girl to school, along with the money and now I'm back in trouble with D.C.F.S. This time I didn't go to jail nor did they do a total investigation. As a matter of fact, the case was dropped after doing a home visit. (Talk about Grace & Mercy). The heat was off me for a while. Now the very game that I was into began to "bite me in the butt".

The Biggest Pay Back

One day, when he was only seven years old, my son was outside playing when he witnessed a young man walk up to a group of boys and give them all a bag of dope (cocaine). He told them to sell it and he would be back to get the money. My son, naïve to the game, comes upstairs and brings it to me. I started going off and cursing like a sailor. I gave my girl a call, who I worked with at the lounge, and told her the situation. Her man had territory over in my hood and got the situation under control. Now it is obvious that my lifestyle had become a generational curse.

During the times that I hung out with Mr. Y, I found myself ending up at the police station in lockup, a lot. The drug scene was getting difficult due to the areas we were hanging out in and the people we were associating. Only by the grace of God, I was being released. However, the last go round wasn't that simple. We were pulled over after being out all night. We were cited for only carrying one pistol. However, I had mine strapped to my thigh. When the female cop patted me down, she missed it because of my big fur coat. We were all escorted into the police car. Me and a young lady were handcuffed in opposite hands, so I was able to get the gun off my thigh. Mr. Y was able to convince the young lady to take the heat for his pistol. I slipped mine off my thigh and pushed it into the back seat of the police car. I wonder what happened to that gun.

FREEDOM IN THE WRONG WAY

I want those who are reading this book to know that when God has a plan for your life, no devil in hell can stop it. Yes, the devil will make his ways of life look good to the point that you will go to the extreme to do them but that's when God will step in. His word tells us in Isaiah 59:19 that when the enemy comes in like a flood, He (God) will put a standard against it. God was putting a standard in my way, called the police, to stop the goals of the enemy regarding my life.

Anyway, Ms. Too Tall and I were slowing down somewhat in a different way. We were getting all the cocaine we wanted but we were not in the streets as much.

As time progressed, I began to find out about things going on in the building that I lived in on Coles. There was a young woman who lived on the first floor who was a druggie. Some kind of way, I befriended her. Then the borrowing of the toilet tissue, toothpaste and household products started. I would supply her with these items because of her habit. Now I got high too, so I was no better than she was. Seen days where my lights were out because I would forget to pay the bill or the house phone would be turned off. I was just as much of a nut case as her but some kind of way, I felt different.

Anyway, I sold her some dope on credit and she didn't pay me back and talked smack behind it. Yes, we argued because I did the stupid by giving her drugs knowing that she didn't have it to give back. This must have been my way of getting rid of her because as we were arguing, I was eating one of my homemade "fiya" (that means really good) salads and jumped through her living room window and broke my salad bowl in her face. Rage had built up from years of anger and now due to the lifestyle that I was living it started coming out. I was displaying a monster that God never created me to be. She moved after that and hadn't seen her since.

As time moved forward, it was time to move. I began to apartment hunt and found a place on 77th and Cornell. I was still in contact with Neicy from 74th and Coles. She came and stayed with me for a while and then, another journey happened in my life.

FREEDOM IN THE WRONG WAY

Chapter Six

The Shifting...

I'm still working at 80th and Halsted but due to my neighbor, Neicy, from 74th and Coles living with me, I started to hang out in the 100's. A particular area in Chicago from State Street to Loomis and from 111th Street to 127th Street, were call the Wild 100's. We called it that because that area was crazier than the "loony tunes".

MR. Z

Neicy was dealing with a married man and I would just go for the ride. The scenario was different and laid back. On the other hand, I pretty much started dealing with a different type of man. I found myself engaging with a man who didn't get high but every now and then. We didn't drink like that either, so now I'm staying sober even while I'm working. I would drink but not to get drunk. So, I was changing. He was a sweetie pie but the relationship didn't last long and it ended in a good way. The relationship actually helped me because I slowed down, tremendously, in drugging and drinking. This was my Mr. Z.

When that relationship was over and I got bored, so I started back running the streets. I found myself hanging out with a bunch of dikes. Today, to be politically correct these groups of women are called Lesbians. The devil had a trap set which God didn't allow to go forth. I loved men too much for that. Anyway, this group of women became my best customers and would come in on my slow nights and spend about for hundred dollars on the bar and tip me between, one hundred to one hundred and fifty dollars. We got to be pretty tight.

Lady S, who was the madam or shall I say, the head ring leader or the "Queen" became pretty tight with me. We exchanged numbers and I would see the clan on my nights to work. The owner, Mr. X, was pissed because our relationship had slowed down and accused me of being a dike. That was the biggest joke ever. One night, Lady S felt like she wanted to die and that her only option was suicide. Well, the night she decided to go forth with her plan, she called me. I was knocked out sleep. WHAT SLEEP…ARE YOU SERIOUS? I TOOK TIME OUT TO SLEEP…..Don't Judge Me….I kept her on the phone long enough to get the right people there and she did live and not die. I was on the phone for what seemed like forever. I never heard from her again.

This is where the devil thought he was going to get me tied up in lesbianism but God said not so.

I finally was tired of 80th and Halsted and quit. After six years, I quit! 80th and Halsted was my world but yes, I was gone. To keep income coming in, I started working at a lounge on 89th and Ashland. It was truly a hole in the wall and it had a car wash connected to it. I was miserable there. I stayed there two months. I quit right after New Year's. The owner was a jerk and cheap. I was tired of 80th and Halsted. Didn't know where I was going was a disaster. I laid low for a while, living off my Have Mercy check and started hanging out more with my girlfriend out South.

MR. AB

In the meantime, I start dealing with this fine man with brown skin and a long ponytail. Let's call him Mr. AB. He was very well known in the streets. He started showing me around in his spots. I began to go in the elite sets in town, jazz clubs that carried a mature crowd. He would even take me to 80th and Halsted just to show me off, as if I was his prized possession, to a crowd whom I had already had roots. We would order top shelf cognac along with fine wine. We were a hot item for a while but then he stole some money from me and totally disappeared off the map. I couldn't find that joker nowhere. It was probably best because my intentions were to kill him.

I found a job on 123rd and Halsted and worked there for a hot minute. This bar was slow and dreary even on the weekends; I don't even care if it was a party jumping. It was the pits. Eventually, I went back to 80th and Halsted and wiggled my way back into working there. It only took a year before I was gone, again. The scenery of people began to change and I was looking for something different. Seven years of ups and downs and then the door closes. 80th and Halsted was completely out of my life. I began to feel differently about the place. I felt like that was it. Not knowing that God was in the midst of this.

Shifting is what I call it. (The door God closes, can't no man open. The number 7 is the number of completion).

MR. AC

Another journey started in my life as I took another break from the bar scene. I was still hanging out with my girlfriend when I met this guy who was a caddy to a golf player. This golf player was also a bigtime drug dealer. We are talking state to state trafficking. The Caddy was a smooth talker and literally took care of my children and me. He pulled me out the streets and was talking marriage. Now he wasn't the best looking but the money overrode everything. (Money is the root of all evil when using and getting it in the wrong way). This time I wasn't selling drugs.

We were together for about a year or so and then the madness began. We were driving and all of a sudden, he knocked the pure mess out of me for no reason. That relationship was an entrapment and I didn't see it coming. Everything started going downhill with him. He was Mr. AC. I wanted out but didn't know how to get out. He had spent some money he wasn't supposed to and we had to take the greyhound out of town. We went to Colorado to escape a hit that he thought was out on him. In the meantime, I had to get a safe haven for my children. So he spoke with the Man (his boss) and he was able to come back to Chi-town.

He tried to get it together. In the meantime, I was trying to figure out how to get out of this madness. I lost my place on 77th

and Cornell, so I started living with my mom, only for this nut to stalk me. The first time I had him arrested after jumping on me, I put an order of protection against him. His mother contacted me and asked not to have her son locked up. I went to court and dropped the charges.

I didn't go back to him but he started stalking me again and beat me up. I went back to the police station on 13th Street and had another order of protection put on him. It didn't matter because whenever he could, Mr. AC would find me and beat me. Everywhere I went I was watching my back. Went and got a pistol and said, "If this man puts his hands on me, again, I'm gonna kill him."

The whole time I had the gun on me, he never showed up but as soon as I released the gun, he was back on the scene. The last stalk came when he followed me to my mom's apartment building. Some kind of way he got into the building. I was coming out of mom's apartment and he pushed his way in. He took the telephone cord, wrapped it around my neck and tried to choke me with it. I was fighting him back with all I had. We literally tore up my mom's place. He saw that he couldn't kill me so he ran out the apartment. My mom was at work. I called her and told her what happened; I also called the police. They ran his name and saw the order of protection tagged to him and the hunt was on.

My mom was furious at him. He forgot that my mom worked for the police department. Enough said. I put my clothes on and went to the bar where my mom was pouring whiskey on the weekends and had quite a few drinks. That incident blew my mind. Never saw him again nor heard from his mom.

God's hand was upon my life even when I didn't know Him. It reminds me of the word of God in II Thessalonians 3:3, "But the Lord is faithful. He will establish you and guard you from the evil one." Hallelujah!

After the drama cooled down, my sister who was working on 80th and Halsted, Ms. Too Tall, found me and said she was working at a new joint, which was a bar. Couldn't believe it. So, I began to go where she's working.

MR. AD

In the meantime, I found a job working on 87th and Kenwood, saved my money and found me a place on 69th and Peoria. I got the kids back and started putting my life back together. Due to the previous relationship I was in, my cousin, who has gone home to be with the Lord, began to chaperone me around. He would pick me up and take me to work and bring me home. I thank God for him because he was my angel. During this time of my life, I was drowning myself in Martell and a little cocaine, not much because where I was working; it wasn't that type of clientele. For a while, I was by myself but then, I felt like it was time for me to get back into a relationship so I hooked up with a guy who was a musician with a blues band. As I said before, the lounge I was working in was a different type of club with a different type of clientele. As time went, we got into a deep relationship and we began to shack for a minute. So, here I go again with the fighting and arguing due to him drinking and drugging. He disappeared for a while, so I was not seeing anyone. He was my Mr. AD.

One night I decided to go out on a binge. I stayed out all night long until about 6am. I was high as a kite and there was no man, no drugs, and not even a drink for me to entertain. I was watching T.V. at 8am on a Sunday morning. I turned the channel and stumbled on a station called WCIU and saw Bishop Brazier and the Apostolic Church of God. I was sprung for real but I heard a man talking about a man who loves you in spite of you. In the mist of my madness, I felt something that I desired for so long in my life and that was LOVE. That following Sunday I got up and took my kids to 6320 South Dorchester on January 31, 1991 and got baptized in Jesus Name. Another journey started in my life.

Chapter Seven

Backslidden...

When this journey began, I was still working on 87th and Kenwood as a bartender. On Saturday nights, I would have a couple of cocktails to allow my night to function. I would get off at 2a.m., go straight home and be right back up for 8:40 am worship service. It felt good being in the house of the Lord. I even tried to make New Members classes but it was truly a conflict because of my work schedule, so that was out.

Anyway, I would go to church consistently but then my Sundays in the house of the Lord began to diminish. First, it was every other Sunday and then once a month, then not at all.

See the enemy knew that I was hearing the word and like seeds, it was being planted but I wasn't strong enough to hold on to what I was hearing.

I was in the position like the verse in Matthew 13:4, in which, seeds were being sewn but the birds came and ate them. As a result, my journey in the house only lasted six months. While still employed at the lounge, I began seeing the young man that was in the band, again. Then the drama started all over. The last incident started with us after Mr. AD and I got into it; we got physical and he pushed me off the second floor porch, which caused me to go to the Emergency Room because of the fall. Had to take x-rays and the sort and was released. I came out with a serious limp. Satan tried to kill me again but because of the Blood of Jesus that was shed on Calvary, I am still here. Glory to God!

The owner of the lounge husband talked much smack. He made sure he put it out there that someone had kicked my behind. What he was saying was true but had no proof. The lie I had circulated was that I was robbed coming from work. In the meantime, I put the word out on Mr. AD to have him seriously hurt. He disappeared and I never saw him again.

I decided to leave that lounge and work with my girlfriend Too Tall on 89th and Ashland. My customers at that place of employment were devastated but staying there wasn't healthy for any of us. So now, I was by myself, which was cool. Ms. Too Tall and I were hanging pretty much because we were both single and "not interested in a relationship". Then she met a young man in her life who took up a lot of her time. I was by myself, chilling for a while until she introduced me to her man's brother and then another journey began; the journey to really discovering me.

MR. AE

This journey in my life rocked my world both, naturally and spiritually. Naturally, I encountered a relationship with a man that took me on a roller coaster ride and spiritually, the experience called life took me back into the presence of God. It took me seven years to get to this point. (Seven is the number of completion).

I began a relationship with a man I will call AE. He was married to a woman he had many children with. This relationship started as a "see you when I can" but turned into a straight love affair. When we first met he acted shy and laid back.

Now laid back he was but shy? Please!

We began dating, seeing each other on the days that I worked. That lasted about a month. I had the pleasure of meeting this man on my job. He was a customer of mine. Before we dated, there were many men trying to see who was going to get a shot at me. Unfortunate for them, I was not interested in any because of the ordeal I just came out of. One was even a firefighter! I turned him down for my own personal reasons. The class of people that came in wasn't a thuggish crowd. Yes, even the drug dealers that were there were very low-key but I knew who they were.

Oh yeah, my stay on 69th and Peoria was more than something to be reckoned with. It was where my son broke his foot although two hospitals stated it wasn't. I pursued differing results until a hospital finally agreed with me because my son couldn't walk. The last hospital took an MRI, which proved that it was broke. This was where my son, also broke his arm playing basketball trying to slam-dunk on a boy who was already six feet tall. It was even where my son learned how to cut hair. Also, where a gang of boys jumped my son. My daughter, my son and I went chasing after them because they wanted his gym shoes. The following day I went up to the schools to find them and they all were arrested on charges of Mob Actions.

This was where my daughter started dating a young man who was 25-years-old while she was only fifteen and I had to go after him with my pistol. This was even where I took my daughter to a restaurant for breakfast and an older man in his fifties approached her like I was not standing there and when I told him I was her mother, he said, "Who asked you? I don't care."

I had to leave the restaurant. Some may feel that my lifestyle was why the man felt like it was okay to approach her but I disagree. The devil thought he had a trap set but God intervened on my behalf. My children had to go through three different gang territories to get to school. This was where I took all the kids candy money along with the rent and tips, gambling on those slot machines they have in those lounges, and then had to go to the after hour joint where they were playing cards in Bid Whist to get it back (I mean recover all). This was where I would make a mean bar-b-que dinner happen and my daughter would get her hustle on by selling plates for five dollars. Ah but this was the place where I could afford a three bedroom for four hundred and fifty dollars.

69th and Peoria was a journey but it was a well-taught lesson. You may be able to get a good price; however, what qualities are you sacrificing to get the deal? Yes, I have many sins but I'm grateful that the bible lets me know in 1John 1:9: But if we confess our sins to Him. He is faithful and just to forgive us our sins and to cleanse us from all wickedness.

Continuing on the journey with Mr. AE, our relationship was getting closer, so he starts coming by the house. He was mild mannered to the kids and they liked him.

To unite our relationship, to make it official, he came by my house one day and we had sex. It was different. He was loving, gentle and compassionate with it. I was like, "Who is this man?" See, he wasn't a fly dresser but when he cleaned up he was fine. He wore shabby clothes because he was a working man. Never had a legit employed man before so this was going to be a new experience for me. He was a smooth talker and introduced me to people who knew how to party without being rowdy. I was like, "Wow, I can do this!" As time goes along, Mr. AE began to spend more time with me to the point that he was at home with me more than his own family. I gave him possession of the house by giving him keys. We became a hot item.

Finally, my Section 8 number came through and I was able to abandon 69th Street. My daughter was in her sophomore year of high school and my son was entering middle school. When I told my Landlord that my Section 8 came through, they were pissed because I was moving out of their building.

Harvey, Illinois was our new home. I found a three-bedroom apartment out there. I was renting from a white man who was a private owner. The place was on 154th and Honore Avenue. I loved that apartment. It was beautiful. The owner of the rental asked my denomination and I told him Pentecostal. I hadn't been to church in over a year or more. I still believe today that answer was my key of entry. (At the Name of Jesus, every knee has to bow).

Mr. AE helped me move out there. He enjoyed it because it was his getaway. I was still working on 89th and Ashland, not knowing how I was going to get to work but I knew that if I got there, I would get back home because of AE.

Transferring of the kids' education was something else. My son wasn't a problem but by my daughter was already in high school and it set her back. The education system was different than the city, so I had to leave her at the school she was attending. At first, it was a struggle because she had early classes and I had to have her on the bus stop by 6a.m. I had to walk her there because 154th Street was the strip for hookers. After a while, I stopped walking her to the corner and she was never harmed.

I finally got adjusted to Harvey. My cousin wasn't too far from me. She lived about four blocks away in the town of Riverdale. I tell you about those South Suburbs, too close for me. Out the back door and down the street, you were in another city.

MR. AF

Anyway, by this time, Mr. AE helped me move but wasn't out there as frequently as he was when I lived in the city. In order for me to get me back and forth, he bought me a little Dodge Charger. So up and down the highway of Interstate-57 I would roll. Then, there would be times that he would disappear from me for weeks. I would begin to feel a little lonely. Since he was married, that gave me the opportunity to roam the streets. I would dibble dabble with my cousin for a hot minute here and there but I began doing my own thing. I began to encounter a relationship with the AF. We became quite an item, too. I would meet with him after 2a.m. when I got off from work. Nothing serious with us. Just something to do until AE came back around. I had to respect that he was married and my time. I didn't sit at home and wait for him to show for the most part. After all, he did have keys so he would show up when he was available.

One night, while I was out with AF having a great old time drinking cocktails, I ran into one of AE's partners at the same lounge. He informed me that AE was on his way there and knew that he liked me a lot. I had to shift my seat and pretend that I was having a drink alone. He came and was shocked that I was there and we began to party like everything was all good. One thing did change after that, AE started coming around a lot more and my relationship with the AF diminished. I do recall before the relationship ended that me and AF were at this hotel and I tell you it was luxurious. It was truly a girl's desire. I was in the mix, hanging downtown and everything. He got me in a place where I thought it was going to be going on and NOTHING! I was so disappointed. The image that he carried would have a woman thinking that he had it going on sexually, as well. It was really "deception" and that's one of Satan's traps. (Daughters of the Most

High God, it's so important to know your worth. You are more than a good time sexually. You are a child of God; His daughter; a Queen.) In my mind, it appeared that because this man had everything going on, on the outside with the women and such, that he was just as good, intimately. Unfortunately, that wasn't the case. Now I'm not saying what I was doing was right because at this point of my life, I still hadn't established a relationship with God. I was still satisfying my flesh. I had to call AE to finish off what had been started. I literally left AF there. I was too blind to see that what mattered was that a man love me and treat me right and that is what true love is about. Some woman would be right for AF, just not me, especially not at that time in my life.

Suddenly, I began playing the Little Miss Homemaker to AE because he "smelled a rat". Why the sudden change? I clearly don't know. Maybe he and his wife were having arguments, again. I couldn't get rid of him at this time. His visits were very frequent but when he did stay home, I would kick it with my cousin. So as I'm out there doing my thing big time, a tragedy hits. February 17, 1993, my son was diagnosed with Juvenile (Type 1) Diabetes. Diabetes is a disease that attacks the pancreas, which causes it not to function properly to release the insulin that is needed in your body to break down the sugar that is obtained from starches that we eat along with other things. (I learned this information after my son was diagnosed. It is also hereditary. It will skip one generation and hit the next. So the disease came from the DNA of his Dad's grandfather).

My son had been sick for a week with what I thought was a cold. I was pumping him with Nyquil but then he began vomiting. I lived down the street from a hospital, so I took him to the ER. Well, they told me he had "Sugar". I was naïve to that term so I asked them what "Sugar" was. To make a long story short, I was almost arrested and sent to jail for child neglect. The doctors thought I was being a dismissive mom but Praise God for nurses who believed me. They rushed him from that hospital to another hospital that had a children's ICU. When we arrived, the hospital was closed but they let us come in. I thank God for what they did for us because my son was slipping into a diabetic coma. His sugar level was almost a 1000. After staying there with him for a week in ICU, he finally got it together and was placed in his own room for another week. During the first week, the hospital couldn't put me out but when we reached the second week I was able to go home with ease. I had my cousin overseeing my daughter. Here again, was the shifting of God in my life trying to get my attention. Now another journey starts in my life.

My son's diet had to take a complete turnaround. Here we couldn't eat what we used to eat and all healthy food had to come into the house. Our eating schedule was even affected because he had to eat at certain times of the day. It took him a while to adjust to his new lifestyle. His disobedience in following the new diet and times kept me practically living in the hospital with him. Even with the medical card helping pay the bills and the free hospital, many of the other hospitals still charged me. I ended up with over seventy-five thousand dollars in medical bills. Those bills accumulated fast and I ended up filing bankruptcy years later. This journey took me for a loop mentally and caused my daughter to feel like she was less favored. Childhood disputes occurred often between the two. Even to this day, one feels I loved the other more.

As time progressed, my son adjusted and life finally seemed to be getting back on track until he decided he didn't want a new needle to shoot his insulin with. He caught an infection in his thigh and the free hospital (Cook County) had to do surgery. The infection had to be cut out and the healing process went like this: I had to clean the wound. I needed to pack it with gauze so that it could heal from the inside out. My son actually made a nurse out of me. Because of him, I know how to read hospital charts, take blood pressure, and I learned about mm's and cc's. During that season with my son, AE couldn't handle the pressure and didn't really come around until the smoke cleared.

More time went by and the journey continued, then I stopped working on 89th and Ashland and started working at a lounge on 97th and Halsted. I wonder if it is still in existence. That was the first lounge I ever worked at and didn't sleep with anyone.

My God, what an accomplishment!

I worked there a long time. I would catch the Pace bus there and AE would come pick me up but I ended up quitting the place. By this time in my life, my car was broken down and sitting in front of the house. I was out of work for a while and ended up working back on 89th and Ashland. It was time for my daughter to graduate from high school. She got herself a telemarketing job after classes so she could pay for her prom and graduation.

While all of this was happening and after she achieved her mission and prepared for College at NIU, my mind was heading in another direction. I was getting tired of the bar scene and I started actually thinking about getting myself a job as a bus driver. My cousin, who I mentioned earlier, had already been with the company for a while and pulled me in as a bus aide. Now this job required a drug test, which I knew I was going to fail because I was reeking of cocaine.... (the overflow, the aftermath, don't matter how you look at it). So, I had to go old school and find out how I was going to get these drugs out my system. That is where Aloe Vera Juice came in. Now at this time of the game, people were using other people's urine to get away with drops but in my case, we had to pee in a cup, in a facility with no doors. So there wasn't any swapping, cheating, or nothing going on like that. This meant I had to clean myself up. Now another journey begins.

Chapter Eight

The Shift...

THE SHIFT

Now there was a shift taking place in my life. I was clean from drugs because of the new career I was embarking upon. I went and filled out the application to become a bus aide at this bus company that is still in operation today. There was a discrepancy in hiring me because you could smell the Martell cognac coming out my pours but the company went on and hired me because of my cousin's reputation and consent. It really pays to know good people who are good at what they do. The bus company had a required procedure going on by which your name could be pulled randomly to go and pee in a cup for drug testing. Many people were being fired because cocaine was found in their urine. Now mind you the policy stated these tests were random. Guess what ya'll! My random was every month. That was God's way of keeping me clean; "Deliverance is the children's bread". That was my rehab.

I was my cousin's Bus Aide and they had us both on the worst bus pick up ever. The bus company considered it as the EMH's (Educable Mentally Handicap) or (Special Ed) bus but all these children really were looking for was love but some of them did want a challenge. I could relate. I was their aide and became familiar with them.

After finishing the school year out, I wanted to become a bus driver. That's what my cousin wanted me to do in the first place. I began reading the necessary books but that wasn't enough for me. So, I took a leave of absence from the job and went to another bus company who gave hands on training. After six weeks of training, I was able to go and take the CDL test. That test was no joke. I failed it twice but when the third time came around, I passed. I was a happy camper. I even asked someone else that had their license to take the test and they failed, too. After passing the road test, I went back to my original job, presented the license and told them what I did. They were a little upset because it was their sister company. I didn't know, I just did what I had to do. They went on and allowed it. Guess what! I got assigned to the group of kids that I was an aide to....funny right. Tell me about it.

Remember, earlier I told you a few of those kids wanted a challenge? Well when they saw that I was their bus driver, one threatened to take my watch. He was the Ring Leader. I politely told him that if he tried that he was "gonna get the worse *&% whooping" that he should have been getting at home. We became the best of friends, even to the point that when he would get in trouble in school, he would have the school call me instead of his parents. I was the intervention. Then there was this other kid that I remember well, he really tried me to the point that I had to pull the bus over and was really getting ready to put my hands on him and he jumped off the back of the bus. I didn't see that kid anymore after that. Didn't have any more problems with the kids after that. Guess what! The following year, I requested to be their bus driver and they were excited for me to be there. My job, on the other hand, thought I was crazy but this was the will of God through

Christ Jesus. Getting those in line who didn't know Christ, including me.

Being a bus driver was the bomb for me. It was my first real job. I enjoyed the hours. I had my car but it began to be a problem. Every other week I was investing in it. Some weeks I couldn't afford to pay to get it worked on, so I would hike it to work by foot, which was a great little walk. I had to walk from Harvey to South Holland. For those who are reading this book and know about the Chicago south suburban area, that could be a long and dangerous walk. Well, I ran into danger one morning while I was walking to work. I decided to take a short cut down a side street to get to the bus company faster. It was more of a dirt road than a street with a lot of weeds and stuff. Anyway, a car drove up on me that was filled with men. I could feel the trouble coming and I took off running. This is a gift called discernment. The car couldn't catch me and I never stopped running until I got to the job. I never walked down that way again. Death was on me but God! I had angels surrounding me.

Well during this time of my life, my cousin decided to move out of the suburbs and she found a house out in the 100's. Now if any one who is reading this book from Chicago knows that the 100's is crazier than that thang. She just happened to meet the Landlord to the house next door and told him about me. After my Section 8 papers cleared, off to the Southside I went and there started another journey in my life. Things were always changing.

Chapter Nine

The Prodigal...

MR. AG

Well this was the journey that brought it on home, back to my Father's house. We moved to 120th and Steward Avenue I tell you the experiences there was more than one could bear but God. I started working at the bus company full time and got elevated to working with PACE Mobile to pick up passengers. I was no longer doing school bus routes. I was making more money and doing midday shifts, which led into some evening shifts.

At this point of my life, Mr. AE had started to fade from the picture for a while. He was stopping by occasionally and it was understood that when he would disappear that he would be doing the family thing. This time he was gone a little longer than normal. So, I really started hanging out with my cousin who lived next door. We would hang out at a lounge on 89th and Stony Island. She was well known there and due to her association, I was put in the mix. At this time in my life I was no longer pouring whiskey or being a Bartender. I had officially retired. It felt good to just go and sit on the other side of the bar and party without reporting in. I was single for a while before being introduced to Mr. AG. He was a nice looking young man, who was single and had a legit job. We began spending a lot of time together but he didn't move in. My kids were cool with him.

He began taking me out to other surroundings other than clubs and lounges. He created other things for us to do like go to the racetracks, have picnics, and when seasons changed we would go to shows and different things. He was more of a family man. It had gotten to the point that when you saw him, I was there as well. One thing I can say is that when I got into a man, I was into him and he had my undivided attention. It had gone on so far that folks thought we were married. At least that's the lie we would tell. Our body chemistry did work well together. We would have our gatherings and then we would have our getaway moments.

There was this moment that him and I were getting away when I was still driving my charger. That car had seen some days but after getting a whole new exhaust system put under that car and getting shocks, she ran like a kitten. Anyway, on our little getaway night, a 1993 Lincoln Town Car hit my Charger from the rear. My car was a two door and a hatchback. That entire big car came through the back of the seats into the passenger and driver. My God! After getting the other car driver's info, me and my guy were sore from the hit but still went to the hotel, anyway. When that Monday came, I reported the accident to the insurance company and my car was "totaled".

Now that was the second accident that my car had been in. The first one almost took my younger and older cousins out. Another Lincoln hit me from behind on the expressway. In this go around, the driver of this car didn't have any insurance so I had to sue my own insurance company, which didn't come out too well because I got another jacked up car, a Buick, with a lousy grand as a down

THE PRODIGAL

payment. I spent more than that getting the Dodge fixed, constantly. I just didn't have any luck with Lincolns.

So now another journey began in my life because Mr. AE wanted to come back home in my life. He started coming around the lounge that Mr. AG and I were hanging out at. What a mess! During this journey, I was caught between two men. One, I was not sure whether I wanted to go back to and the other, I didn't want to let go of but he had already made the decision for me because he had another woman. It was painful but that was the drawing card pulling me into a direction, I had not a clue I was going into.

I began drinking, trying to fill a void in my life (even though I had a man with me) and trying to get rid of depression. I ended up drinking a half of gallon of Martell cognac a day. When I was at work, I was drinking and driving. I would be drinking my Budweiser beer while waiting on passengers. I was trying to kill the pain I was carrying. Then I lost my job with Pace and lost my CDL's.

I was trying to get it together and then, Mr. AE moves back into my life. So, I slowed down with the drinking and tried to start my own business called Y-Tell. It was a cologne business. I did a road trip to try to sell but I did not make not one transaction. That company didn't last long at all. Then to top it all off, I lost the house on Steward. Everything that I was trying to accomplish was turning to garbage. Everything in my life was going in a spiral downhill. With no other outlet, I called my mom for me, my two children and my man to stay in a one bedroom. This started another journey in my life.

At this point, we all moved in with my mom. At first it was cool and the gang. I know those who are reading this book are probably saying, "You got a lot of nerves asking your mother, of all people, can all ya'll move into her place." All I can say is certain situations call for drastic measures. But what else can I say? After putting my stuff in storage and just bringing in clothes, everything was tight. Then it started to get uncomfortable for mom but she dealt with it. After a while, my mom made a call for my daughter to stay with a friend. Then, it was just me, my son and Mr. AE. Everything seemed to be going well although the process of moving out was taking a little bit too long for mom. She began leaving little notes over the bathroom sink to turn the water off along with not touching her food. During that time, I wasn't working so Mr. AE was the income. He left his family and began to provide for mine.

I was trying to find a place that would accommodate my Section 8. A door would not open anywhere. I was so frustrated that I made a phone call to a psychic hotline. (Don't ya'll sit there as if you don't know what I'm talking about…lol). I was trying to find some answers. On the weekends Mr. AE and I would go out. I was truly a drunk and I lived up to the name. We would come back to the house and he would want to make love to me while my son was in the room. We got away with it for the most part. However, one night we came in while I was drunk and I started having a flash back of my dad trying to fondle me and I screamed out, "Don't touch me!"

Well that sent AE for a loop because he didn't know about my secrets. Then there was another night I came in drunk and cussed AE totally out because that is what champagne and cognac will do for you. But the finale was when he, my mom and I was at this bar on 89th and Ashland, and we were partying good. I had one too many drinks, went to stand up on the bar stool and hit the floor. I went to the house and was sick as a dog the next day. I vowed I would not do that again and I didn't. My son had seen me drunk a many a day but not like that and asked my mom what was wrong with me and mom replied, "A hangover."

Time progressed and still I had no place. It was February of 1997 and I got a job being a security guard. I was working some crazy hours but it was a job. It had gotten to the place that mom couldn't take it anymore so she told us we had a few weeks to move. My son was in his last year of high school and we had nowhere to go. This situation was another drawing card calling me back to place in which I had no clue where it was leading.

My son stayed with mom for a minute and AE and I went to stay in a building where there was no heat, no refrigerator, no stove, and no hot water but it was a roof over our heads. We had a TV, a heater, and a hot plate. We put our food on the back porch to stay cold and cooked it in a toaster oven. It was a drawing card that he had not a clue about, either.

Now most of you who are reading this are saying she is crazier than that thang to live like that but at the end you will see why I had to go through this journey. As I was working and living under those conditions, something caught my attention while watching TV one Sunday morning. When I took this job, I went in telling them I didn't do Sundays. Why I went in like that, I don't know but I did. Anyway, one Sunday I was looking at television and Bishop Brazier from the Apostolic Church of God was preaching. The same man that was used to draw me in before. I was back in his face again. The inside of me was jumping for joy. My son had finally moved over in the building with me. The month of April rolled around and a breakthrough came. I got a place out in the South Suburbs. Would you believe back in Harvey? Only it was called East Harvey.

We got the place in May and moved in. We went and got our possessions out of the storage unit on West 111th Place by Cicero Avenue, I started going back to bible study on Wednesday nights and when June 1st 1997 came, that Sunday, I made my way back to the house of the Lord. When I walked down the aisle, after everyone had given their lives over to Jesus, Bishop (that's what everyone called him) said to me in front of a church full (because the Dorchester Sanctuary holds at least three thousand people), "You know Jesus loves you?" and I said, "Yes Sir." Then he said,

"Welcome home!" and gave me a godly hug in front of the congregation. Now how did Bishop know that I was a Prodigal? Only God! Yes, this Prodigal child made it back to the House of the Lord Jesus Christ.

Chapter Ten

The End of a New Beginning...

JESUS' LOVE

So after my return of being in the House of the Lord and going back to church I began to realize who I am. My deliverance began to take place. I started breaking free from the family secrets of rejection; from a mother's love; and the mental, physical and sexual abuse from the uncles to the father, which caused me to live a broken, unhealed and unfulfilled life. It caused me to have children thinking that I could give them what I never had, only to bring them into my chaotic life filled with pain, which caused the cycle to continue and it was all a part of the enemy's plan. You may be wondering what elements of my life were part of his wicked plan? Let's take a look:

- ✓ Drug Addiction
- ✓ Physical Abuse
- ✓ Alcohol Addiction
- ✓ Sexual Addiction
- ✓ Low Self-Esteem
- ✓ Lesbianism
- ✓ Suicidal Thoughts
- ✓ Depression
- ✓ Generational Curses
- ✓ Unforgiveness

These were the tools that he used and wanted me to be bound in but the chains, the fetters and yokes were no match for God. God's word says in John 8:32, *"You shall know the truth and the truth shall set you free"*.

I had come into the truth that after all I had been through and all I had done, I was forgiven from the Almighty Father!

Jesus wanted me to learn of His Redemption, letting others know that they too, can be saved from sin, evil or even themselves because Jesus loves them just that much. Everyone has a purpose for living. That is why there is a need for your birth. With me, it was destined for me to declare the Word of God. The enemy came to steal, kill and destroy and his mission was to get me as a child, to shut me down but God said I would live and not die to declare His word.

Yes, my first journey after being back into the house of the Lord, Jesus Christ was to share my salvation process with Mr. AE. I started being active in the church. I started getting into things that mattered to the Father. I joined the homeless ministry, two as a matter of fact, which was a drawing card to get me in a place with God. There had come a time when I was a meeting with one of the homeless ministries and the subject came up about living Holy. It was the plan of God. I wasn't married to Mr. AE yet but I was still sexually active with him. At this meeting about Holiness in October of 1997, I became convicted without realizing what was going on in my life. Not only was a change coming about my

THE END OF A NEW BEGINNING

relationship status but I was being called into ministry. I came home as usual but things began to change with me. I didn't want to have sex or make love with him any longer until we got married. I didn't say anything at first but by the time mid-October rolled around, I made it clear to Mr. AE that I wanted marriage. Well early one morning, Mr. AE yanked at my panties. He was in motion to come after his stuff but my body no longer belonged to him. God had begun to do "a new thing" in me (Isaiah 43:19). I never opened my mouth but I begin to pray inwardly asking God not to let him touch me until we were married. See there was still a process that needed to happen with Mr. AE. He was still married. God heard me and he didn't touch me. I have been celibate ever since. That was the first process of deliverance for me.

Then, there came the process of being an Evangelist without knowing it. The more I went to church and came back with what the preacher was saying, the more he started getting interested in God. Remember I told you earlier that a drawing was taking place with him that he couldn't understand? His calling to salvation was here and it was time for him to answer. Well the more I talked about God, about the forgiveness of His Son, Jesus and His love, the more Mr. AE wanted to know. By December of 1997, Mr. AE came to church, heard the gospel from Bishop George Bloomer about how Jesus would forgive even those who were drug addicts. That was the drawing card because it related to him and he was saved that Sunday. I still rejoice because even though we were in mess by living in the same house and he was married to another, God still got the glory out of his life by being saved and filled with the Holy Ghost. Well, it wasn't too long after that when he moved out the bedroom and into the living room. We began to go to church, together.

Now to show you how the devil tried to creep in, my two children were having a problem with Mr. AE being there in the house. He was paying the bills, so he laid down some laws, which both of my children felt they were "grown" so to speak and didn't have to obey. My daughter was out of school but not independent and my son hadn't graduated from high school, yet. One of them decided to call my dad. So, my father made a trip out to Harvey with his controlling spirit and tried to tell me what was going to happen in my house. It did not work. I did not disrespect my father nor did Mr. AE but we did ask him to leave. Another portion of Deliverance took place. No more control. So my daughter moved out the house because I told her she had to pay $75 a month for rent. She threatened to blow up the place but that was just mouth. In the end, just the three of us lived there. It pretty much spoke for itself about who called dad.

FINALLY, ME

February 14, 1998 came and Mr. AE gave me a rose, a box of candy and a card and told me he's leaving for the sake of doing what's right and he would only see me on Sundays. That rocked my world because I never lived by myself. Mr. AE came to church for a minute but by the time March rolled around; he was gone. Then, it was just two of us, me and my son. This process is called Finally Me because I was about to learn about Karen. Who was I? I was in process of learning that I am a child of King Jesus. Hallelujah, Jesus!

My son graduated from Thornton High School and was doing his own thing. Over the summer months, my child had gone buck wild smoking weed and selling it, all at the same time. I came in from church one evening after working all day and my house smelled like a weed factory. I kicked in the bedroom door and told him and his friends they were all going to hell. Look at the transformation that took place in my life. We still laugh at that today.

By the time September came, I received a letter from the Public Aid Office saying they were going to cut out my food stamps for my son. I remember the conversation well. I told them my son was a diabetic and I needed them to feed him. They said access denied and closed the case and cut the stamps anyway. I was disappointed. I sat in the middle of my cousin's living room floor and said, "Well, Jesus, I guess I'm gonna have to trust you with feeding me and my child."

Another process called trust happened because later on that week, without me saying anything to anybody at the church, I got a knock at the door from a church member with bags of grocery flowing from everywhere. God proved Himself again. Yes, the words of Isaiah 43:19 had started to manifest in my life of God doing a New Thing! Never had anyone taken care of me before.

Another journey was happening with me because my son left and went to stay with his dad and I was alone. I was about to learn who God is.

Living by myself was very foreign to me but that was the journey of learning me. I had never been Single. I always had the responsibility of caring for someone other than myself. This was where restoration and healing began in my life. This was where I came to know Jesus as a Provider in a whole different way. This was where I learned about forgiveness. This was where I was being built up. I was about to understand, *Finally, Me*!

I had to get to learn how to love me and in order to learn that I had to learn about the love of Christ. God started taking me on a journey of showing me His love. He began by giving me what I never had and that was the love of a parent. He did things like provide me with clothing. For example, a minister from one of the Homeless Ministries I was in knew I did not have any clothes and the clothes that I dressed up in were for going to the club. She went into her closet and gave me every outfit that she could no longer wear. Then, there came the shoes from another sister in the church. Keeping my hair done, for a while I couldn't afford to get it done although I tried but after a while I went to an old hair dresser who was in the body of Christ and she would give me free hairdo's.

THE END OF A NEW BEGINNING

And when the struggles came, God would send people to put money in my hand at the right time for whatever it was that I needed at that moment. God was showing me that He was there. He was showing me a Real Love.

This takes me to the scripture of 1Corinthians 13:4-7:

Love is patient, love is kind. It does not envy, it does not boast, it is not proud. It does not dishonor others, it is not self-seeking, it is not easily angered, it keeps no record of wrongs. Love does not delight in evil but rejoices with the truth. It always protects, always trusts, always hopes, always perseveres.

I kept myself busy because of the loneliness. There would be times that I would go home and cry and I would ask God why He took AE away from me. I didn't like the feeling that I had of being alone and lonely. There were a lot of long nights of holding my pillow as the tears fell and grabbing my bible because that was as close to God as I was going to get. God understood. He would send a sister in the Lord to hold me in their arms and give me a hug or speak a word of comfort.

All these people of God and activities I was involved with at the church was a part of the process of my deliverance from Mr. A through Z and more. As Prophetess Juanita Bynum would put it, "No More Sheets," was unraveled. God emptied me out, only to be refilled with the love of Christ. This was truly a good couple of years. I had made a commitment to God that I would give Him a year of just He and I, alone. No relationships, just the Lord. I did not know it would be almost 20 years later and there would still be no relationship. I also didn't know that I would find the strength, courage and love to be content in my situation.

As time progressed, I began going into intercessory prayer. It was held on a Friday nights and I was like why not….I partied on Fridays, why not go to church to prayer? It was the same routine just different dance partners. Intercessory prayer was a new journey in my life because this is where I was first filled with the Holy Spirit by speaking in tongues as evidence. Wow, what a feeling! I remember a particular member of the prayer group, who saw and heard me speaking in my heavenly language, saying, "God is having His way." I miss that girl. She has gone on home to be with Lord.

As time progressed, He began to empty my history from me. He was getting rid of the evidence of my past. Every picture, piece of clothing, piece of jewelry that had an attachment to a man went in the garbage. It ended up with about for garbage bags full of things. It wasn't too long after that when I moved back to the city. That was another process taking place. Everything was working for my good (Romans 8:28).

Now that God was doing a work in me, the devil entered again with one of his tricks. I would take naps on the Red Line train after getting off from work because I was tired. It was a long ride from the Westside of Chicago to Harvey. Well this particular day, I went to sleep and began to have a dream of me getting high off the pipe smoking cocaine. I actually felt the effects of it. The dream was so real.

We wrestle not with flesh and blood but principalities, wickedness in high places. (Ephesians 6:12)

I woke up out the dream sweating bullets. I called one of the ministers at their home and they asked did I want them to come and get me. My reply was, "No, I'm alright because Jesus is with me."

His word declared that He would never leave me nor forsake me and He didn't. I overcame that obstacle. Thank you, Jesus!

As I continued to follow the Lord, the soul ties that I had encountered with my children fathers had broken. Glory be to God! (One through death, Mr. E. and the other through the word of God, Mr. D) I was free!

As that journey continued, I took a class called the Fruit of the Spirit. It was a powerful class, taught by a powerful, Holy Ghost filled women of God. The night that I was there, another set up by God took place. I ended up in the middle of the circle and all the prayer warriors were around me praying. Then the instructor facilitating the class that night began to talk about Forgiveness. She asked me who had hurt me in this degree. I answered by saying my dad, Mr. B but then there was also, Mr. AC. (The one who tried to kill me physically at my mom's house). After I cried and cried, snot was everywhere; deliverance had truly taken place that night in the church house.

As time went on, I continued to move forward with my life. I moved to the city and I started taking ministry classes. I began to learn more about me; I was discovering my likes and dislikes. It was like growing up all over again. I went through stages of being Daddy's little girl, to becoming a teen in Him. I was actually hanging out with the sisters from the church like teens are supposed to do instead of what's happening nowadays. I went from being an adolescent in my spirituality to becoming a mature, godly woman in the Lord. As I was also involved in different ministry groups. This was helping me to become who God wanted me to be and to learn of Him more. I had the opportunity to Finally, know Me!

I have learned that obeying my Heavenly Father is the most important thing in my life. I have learned that I still like to go out and have fun but only in a constructive way. Most people believe that living a Christian life is boring and I have to beg the difference. I love dressing conservative and looking like a lady. I still enjoy cooking, unexpectedly. An important aspect for me in this journey of knowing about God's love was being able to forgive. God began to deal with my fears regarding my dad and the child molestation. The devil had me fooled. For years, I thought my Dad's behavior was normal because that is how I grew up. I know I didn't like it but it became a part of my lifestyle. God showed me what real love looked like and that was not it. What my dad and uncles did to me was wrong, that is not how a parent loves their child. I finally confronted my Dad with it and asked him why? His reply was that the people in the bible did it. But I came back and told him that that was a lie and still didn't make it right. God never condoned incest. Be careful because Satan will try to twist the words of the bible for his own benefit. That is why we are told in 2 Timothy 2:15 to "study and show ourselves approved".

You have to know the word for yourself. People can tell you anything. Get your own bible, research, read and reread. Ask questions, take classes and pray. The Word is one of our powerful weapons of warfare. Well, I told my Dad I loved him and he told me the same. I forgave him and another form of deliverance took place. I was just set free from the hand of the enemy regarding Forgiveness. See forgiving isn't for the other person; it's for you to become free within yourself, to be healed in your heart, to receive more from God without hindrances in the way. (Aw, yes, Daughter of Zion, God has much for you to receive from Him and doesn't want anything in the way between you and Him.)

One other thing I did find out about myself was that I love to encourage people and make them laugh because it helps me to find joy about life. Within that laughter, I can also correct in such a gentle way in love that you will know that I'm serious and not playing. Another thing I learned about myself is that I dislike when someone asks for my advice about a situation and then do just the opposite. Then, when their way fails and they come back to me with a sad face, I do not say I told you so but I do feel like I just wasted valuable time. That really annoys me. I also found out that I dislike it when people try to play on my intelligence but I can't say anything until Jesus allows me to open my mouth. God has shown me so much but the main thing that I have come to discover is He is an Amazing God with so much amazing Grace. What a Journey!

If you are reading this book and you are dealing with challenges of low self- esteem, drug and alcohol addictions, or physical abuse because you feel you are not worthy of better, I need you to know that you are worthy. Stop listening to the lies of the devil saying this is the best you can do, I am here to tell you the devil is a liar and the truth is not in him.

But you are a chosen generation, a royal priesthood, a holy nation, a peculiar people; that you should show forth the praises of Him who called you out of darkness into His marvelous light.
(1 Peter 2:9)

You are special to God. You are the apple of His eye.

For those of you who are reading this book and you are caught up in sexual addictions because you feel sex will drown the pain of the misery you're in, or those living a lesbian lifestyle because you couldn't take another abusive relationship from a man, or your self-esteem was broken down by family members and the devil enticed you and said go for it; I'm here to tell you that God is a Deliverer. Deliverance is the children's bread and the only way out is through the Love of Jesus Christ.

Yes, I have loved you with an everlasting love. (Jeremiah 31:3)

For those who are reading this book that are dealing with depression and suicidal thoughts because life has taken you through valleys and dark places that you never imagined: Just know that Jesus can fix it!

The word of God says in Jeremiah 29:11, *"For I know the plans I have towards you which are of good and not evil to bring you to an expected end."*

You have purpose. You were created for the Master's use.

Those who are reading this book and are holding unforgiveness in their hearts because of what they have been through by the hand of someone else, forgive them because it's not for them but for you so that you can move on in life.

If you forgive men when they sin against you, your heavenly Father will forgive you. (Matthew 6:14-15)

I have to tell this story, again because this seemed like the foundation of my journeys with men. After I confronted my Dad about the molestation, he tried to justify the wrong by saying they did it in the bible. Even that horrible lie didn't stop me from forgiving him. (That statement was inaccurate anyway, the bible, never condoned incest or parents sleeping with their children. Look at Satan, how he is the accuser of the brotheren! (Revelation 12:10) When I told my dad that I forgave him and that I still love him and he replied that he loved me, too. Forgiveness released me from the hurt, pain and anguish that the enemy used against me for years.

This evilness that occurred in my life had me to believe that the only love that I was worthy of receiving was by sleeping with every man available; every man that would show any type of attention towards me because my dad showed me the wrong type of attention. All I was looking for was love, real Love. Since that day of my confrontation with my dad, our relationship was reconciled through the power of Jesus Christ. When I decided to forgive my Father, things began to change.

Many strongholds were destroyed because of the simple, effective act of forgiveness. One of those strongholds was fear. Fear of letting my daughter around my dad. Forgiving my dad also allowed me to be able to go to my children who I did so much damage to and ask them to forgive me. I needed forgiveness, as well. My children were angry with me for years. They had every right to be. They weren't able to experience the fullness of God just like I wasn't. Horrible things happened to them in their young life because of me. Do you know God worked that out, too? We reconciled. My daughter and son finally forgave me. With my girl, our relationship turned into a true mother and daughter relationship. My son and I share a bond like a mother and son should. We all have an awesome love for each other. I praise God for deliverance in my mind because I did some crazy things. Don't miss out on your blessings because of someone else's behavior.

There might be someone reading this book who wants to know more about this loving, forgiving Father. You might not be saved, in other words, you may not know Jesus for the pardon of your sins. If you don't, here's an opportunity to give your life to Jesus.

The word of God declares in John 3:16 that *God so loved the world that He gave His only begotten Son that who so ever believe in Him will have eternal life.*

Then in Romans 10:9, *"If you confess with your mouth that Jesus is Lord and believe in your heart that God raised him from the dead you will be saved."*

Then Acts 2:38 says, *"Repent and let every one of you be baptized in the name of Jesus Christ for the remission of sins and you shall receive the gift of the Holy Spirit."*

Get to a church that is preaching and teaching Jesus Christ and when you do so, you will have taken the first step and Jesus will handle the rest. Jesus Can Fix it. He did it for me. Now, I have a new journey that ends and begins with Him as my Lord and Savior. He is leading the journey, directing my path and instructing me on the ways to go. I am confident in the Lord being my head and when people see me, they see Him. It is the best journey I have ever taken and I will rejoice in Him all the days of my life.

The End

ABOUT THE AUTHOR

Prophetess Karen Wright resides in Chicago, Illinois. She is a "Lighthouse to the World", whose purpose is to direct the unknowing to Jesus. She is the founder of Jesus Cares, a transitional housing program for single, homeless women.

Karen is the mother of two, grandmother of five and Spiritual Mother of many. She loves God with her life and firmly believes that **Jesus Can Fix It!**

**For bookings, interviews and more information,
send an email to inspire@blessedpenink.com
and add Karen Wright to the subject line or visit:
www.blessedpenink.com**

www.ingramcontent.com/pod-product-compliance
Lightning Source LLC
Chambersburg PA
CBHW070454100426
42743CB00010B/1609